the Love & Romance TEEN QUIZ BOOK

Also by Annalee Levine, Jana Johnson,
and Arlene Hamilton Stewart:

■ ■ ■ ■ ■ ■ ■

The Teen Quiz Book

the Love & Romance TEEN QUIZ BOOK

Annalee Levine ♥ Jana Johnson ♥ Arlene Hamilton Stewart

Andrews McMeel Publishing

Kansas City

03 04 05 RDC 10 9 8 7 6 5 4 3

ISBN: 0-7407-1988-2

Library of Congress Control Number: 2001087119

Book design by Lisa Martin

**The authors would like to thank
Patricia Rice of Andrews McMeel Publishing
for giving us the opportunity to write this book
and Jennifer Fox for so carefully editing it.**

CONTENTS

■ ■ ■ ■ ■ ■ ■

Chapter Three: Dating

Chapter Four: **All about You**

Chapter Five: **Sticky Situations**

INTRODUCTION

■ ■ ■ ■ ■ ■ ■

We think it's hard enough just being a teenager—what with physical changes, school, the parental figures, and all. But add to that being a teen who falls for another teen, and you've got a fairly endless supply of juicy love and romance issues. As two typical teens, we've been through a lot, and what we haven't experienced directly, our buds have. We know that dreams about guys are a big part of your lives now—that's why we want you to download what we've experienced. From "What Are the Ten Things Guys Want in Girls?" to "'Yikes! My Family Hates Him!' Can True Romance Prevail?" to "Can You Make It Work Long Distance?" from romance styles to prom profiles, we've packed these pages with soul-searching, thought-provoking quizzes that explore the complex world of teen romance.

We hope you have as much fun reading this as we've had writing it—and remember, there aren't too many rules here. If it feels right, it probably is right!

Quiz on,
Annalee and Jana

chapter ONE
CRUSHES

So you think finding a guy to crush on—and to crush on you—is the hard part? Plenty of scary, thrilling, and baffling things come up in the crush relationship stage that need exploring. This is the time to savor the fun you're having and to discover what you should expect from a new guy—and what may be expected of you.

HOW CAN I TELL
if he **likes** me?

Does he . . . or doesn't he? Yes, this is the immortal question that's been on our minds more than anything else except possibly, "Does my hair look good this way?" Especially in romance's first blush, it takes skill to decode signals and signs that your crush's mind is fixing on you. Test your analytic ability by selecting the answer that best fits the question "Does this mean he likes me?"

■ ■

1 As you pass your crush's lunch table, you drop your tray and everything hits the floor. He responds by

__**a.** laughing and then reenacting your trauma for the entire cafeteria's enjoyment.

X **b.** starting to chuckle but stopping before his friends can join in.

__**c.** giggling and hopping out of his chair to help you scoop up the rest of your mac 'n' cheese.

2 Your birthday is a week away and your friends confess they've invited your crush to the party. When he arrives, he

__**a.** says, "You didn't eat the cake yet, did you?" then heads straight for the food.

X**b.** says, "Happy birthday," and hands you a gift.

__**c.** says, "Happy birthday," while hugging you and then hands you a present with a rose.

3 When your teacher assigns a project with the option of choosing a partner, your crush reacts by

__**a.** asking the girl next to him to work together.

X**b.** working on his own.

__**c.** sliding right toward your desk and proposing you work together.

4 On Valentine's Day, your homeroom teacher passes out the carnations the Math Club sold at lunch last week. She hands you yours and one of them is from your crush. Is it

__**a.** white?

X**b.** pink?

__**c.** red?

5 At the Winter Ball, the last love song of the night is about to be played and you desperately hope your crush will ask you to dance. When you spot him, he is

___**a.** dancing with the same girl he has been glued to all night.

___**b.** sitting down massaging his sore feet.

✗ **c.** coming toward you to ask for a dance.

6 When cramming for midterms in the library, you see your star sweetie walk in. Going nuts with the biology questions, you are hoping for some help. He stops and

___**a.** says, "That stuff is so easy. Don't tell me you're having problems with bio."

___**b.** pulls up a chair to chat but soon leaves for his math study session.

✗ **c.** sensing your frustration, he offers to help you and cracks open his book.

7 Just like your daydream promised, you pick up the phone and it's your crush on the line. After catching your breath from excitement, you hear him ask you

__ **a.** if your best friend has a boyfriend.

X **b.** if your best friend has a date to the dance on Friday, because his best friend needs a date.

__ **c.** if your best friend can go with his bud and suggests a double date if you will be his date.

8 At the big Homecoming game, you see your crush in the stands as you are riding by in a float dressed as the school mascot. He sees you and

__ **a.** looks the other way.

X **b.** smiles and keeps talking to his friends.

__ **c.** smiles and waves.

9 Five minutes before class starts, you're frantically searching your locker for the worksheet for math. He spots you fumbling through binders, tossing papers on the floor. He comes over and says

__ **a.** "I hope you are planning on cleaning that mess up."

__ **b.** "Good luck—the bell is going to ring soon."

X **c.** "Can I help you find whatever you are searching for before the bell rings?"

10 At the movies, you and your girlfriends spy your crush with his buddies buying popcorn. Your crush

__ **a.** says to his bud, "We are not sitting with them."

X **b.** comes over and sits in front of you.

__ **c.** offers you some popcorn and asks if he can sit next to you.

SCORING

Mostly A's: ICE KING

Come in from the cold from this guy. He is not putting out the right signals to let you know if he digs you. His bad attitude and rude comments prove he isn't worth your time. Consider finding a new crush, one who will appreciate you for who you are.

Mostly B's: LUKEWARM

This is a tricky situation. Although he might be sending out friendly signs, friendship could be where it ends. Perhaps he isn't sure how he feels. If you decide to go after him, beware!—he could be looking for a friend, not a flame.

Mostly C's: LIGHTING HIS FIRE

This guy is hot after you. He is sending all the right signals that he totally digs you and wants to spend a lot of time together. His body language and clear flirting assure he is ready to take the next step.

what are the
TEN THINGS
GUYS WANT in girls?

On this list below are ten qualities guys dig in girls. Can you spot them? Take this quiz to find out if you're clued in or clueless.

■■■■■■■■■■■■■■■■■■■■■■■■■■■■■■■

Check true or false:

1 Someone who shows she cares.

☒ **TRUE** ☐ **FALSE**

2 A girl who tries to impress him—even if it means pretending.

☒ **TRUE** ☐ **FALSE**

3 A carefree spirit.

☒ **TRUE** ☐ **FALSE**

4 Someone with soul mate potential.

☐ **TRUE** ☒ **FALSE**

5 A gal pal who will hook up.

☒ **TRUE** ☐ **FALSE**

6 Someone who's self-reliant.

☒ **TRUE** ☒ **FALSE**

7 A girl with an independent life from their life together.
☐ TRUE ☒ FALSE

8 A chick with a sense of humor.
☒ TRUE ☐ FALSE

9 Someone who's sarcastic.
☒ TRUE ☐ FALSE

10 A girl who's ambiguous and indecisive.
☒ TRUE ☐ FALSE

11 A mate who exudes confidence.
☐ TRUE ☒ FALSE

12 Someone who shows lots of insecurities.
☐ TRUE ☒ FALSE

13 A girl who bad-mouths others.
☐ TRUE ☒ FALSE

14 Someone who carries lots of baggage from her ex.
☐ TRUE ☒ FALSE

15 A girl who conforms instead of sticking to her own desires.
☐ TRUE ☒ FALSE

16 A flake.
☐ TRUE ☒ FALSE

17 A girl who lacks common sense.
☐ TRUE ☒ FALSE

18 A love who is gullible and believes anything she hears.
☐ TRUE ☒ FALSE

19 A girl whose confidence borders on cockiness.
☐ TRUE ☒ FALSE

20 A material girl.
☐ TRUE ☒ FALSE

ANSWERS

1. **TRUE.** Guys love girls who are willing to put in effort to show they care. Sending a postcard while on vacation or a get-well card will make him feel loved.

2. **FALSE.** Guys aren't into girls who constantly pretend to be someone else. Sooner or later, he will find out who the "real" you is. Being yourself from the start will show him you are sure of yourself, and if he doesn't like you, then you haven't wasted time pretending to be someone else.

3. **TRUE and FALSE.** While some guys are reeled in by a carefree spirit, some are turned off. There is a difference between being a free spirit who goes by her own rules and one who is lazy and inconsistent with her word.

4. **TRUE.** Guys, just like girls, want to find a soul mate in life. There is nothing in the world like a true connection to someone.

5. **TRUE and FALSE.** Some guys are only in it for the thrill of a hookup, but those who want to stick around have more long-term potential.

6. **TRUE.** Guys love girls who are self-reliant and able to be their own person.

7. **TRUE.** Independence can be one of the biggest turn-ons for guys. He'll love the idea that you will have a life outside your relationship with him.

8. **TRUE.** Doesn't everyone want someone who makes them laugh?

9. **TRUE and FALSE.** While some guys are turned on by sarcastic humor, some are turned off by the "in your face" approach.

10. **FALSE.** Guys aren't crazy about girls who can't make decisions. If he asks about a movie or dinner, step up and suggest one you are interested in rather than saying, "It doesn't matter to me, you decide."

11. **TRUE.** Confidence may be the ultimate turn-on. Showing you are comfortable in your own skin and proud of yourself will drive him mad for you.

12. **FALSE.** Insecurities can be overwhelming to a guy. Your constantly fishing for compliments and affirmation can tire out a guy and may make you seem like high maintenance.

13. **FALSE.** No one wants a person who bad-mouths others. Keeping your lips shut will prove you don't have to put others down to make your-self feel good.

14. **FALSE.** Baggage, whether it be emotional or not, from an ex boyfriend can push a guy out the

door. Constantly mentioning good times with your ex or the horrible fights you had will show that you are not ready to move on to another relationship.

15. **FALSE.** Most guys want girls who are unique and stick out instead of those who conform to the standards. Be yourself and your wonderful quirks will intrigue him.

16. **FALSE.** Flakiness will show that you are not confident in your opinions or able to be relied upon. For him to trust you, you must be able to keep your word and have opinions of your own.

17. **FALSE.** Guys want girls who have common sense and are able to make decisions, especially the most basic ones.

18. **FALSE.** If you want to reel in your guy, show him you don't believe everything you hear. Especially with rumors, question what you hear before you believe it and act on it.

19. **FALSE.** While guys are majorly turned on by a true sense of confidence, having too much can turn them away. *No* one wants someone who parades around as the hottest thing ever. You can prove yourself without going overboard.

20. **FALSE.** This may work for Madonna, but it scares most guys off.

Do You Know the
SMOOTH MOVES?

You've decided now is the time to make a move on your crush. Take this quiz to find out if your moves will land him or lose him.

■ ■

Identify A or B as the "smoother move."

1 **You heard your crush may be into you.**

__**a.** You ask your friend to conference-call him so you can hear what he says "firsthand."

✗**b.** You have your friend ask one of his buddies if he digs you.

2 **The teacher just assigned a project for history, your favorite subject.**

__**a.** To include him, you ask to meet him at the library to study.

✗**b.** You encourage him to join your study group.

3 The big dance is coming up and there is no one you'd rather go with than your crush. You

X **a.** muscle up the courage to ask him.

___ **b.** get a friend to ask his friend. Maybe he'll ask you and then you can all go as a group.

4 You saw your friend talking to your crush in the hall. Could it have been about you? To find out, you

X **a.** wait until lunch to ask.

___ **b.** slide a note past him to your bud's desk.

5 Your parents leave for the weekend and you're home alone. Figuring it's the perfect chance to hang with your crush, you

___ **a.** call him but flake out and tell him you're having a party instead.

X **b.** call him and bravely ask if he wants to rent a movie.

6 At the spring carnival, you hear he loves crazy rides. You are freaked by them but get up the courage to ask him to go on the

__**a.** Ferris wheel.

X**b.** roller coaster.

7 After a late-night party, he offers you a ride home. Knowing it's against your parents' rules to ride with him, you

__**a.** jump in—your parents won't know.

X**b.** pass, even though you are dying for a ride.

SCORING

1. A: Beware of the dangerous three-way calling. There is potential for a backfire. While you will get the chance to hear his opinions "firsthand," are you ready for the brutal truth or possible rejection? If you do go for it, remember it is better to find out what you should hear instead of what you want to hear.

B: The middleman can cause obvious complications. For one, that will be another person who knows about your crush. Also, word of mouth could change his answer and possibly misinterpret it, for better or worse.

Our tip: Wait it out until his thoughts about you are clearer, then talk to him yourself. That is the best way to find out how he feels.

2. A: This is a good move—it is casual—but can you really talk at the library?

B: Including him in the group is the smoother move. Just make sure he will pull his own weight. You don't want to be turned off by his lazy attitude toward your favorite subject.

3. A: This move is particularly confident and will show him your initiative and strong sense of self.

B: Although there is a sense of safety in numbers, you could be out of luck. If he doesn't ask you, your friend might be going with his group while you are left out.

4. A: This is the best option. Wait until lunch. Your patience will prove your maturity.

B: Tricky move. Passing a note is a sly move, but past his desk increases the chance of an interception, the ultimate embarrassing move.

5. A: If you do flake out and tell him you are having a party, do not give the impression your house is available for a rager. Never mention, "My parents are away," and "Wanna come over?" in the same sentence. Rather, let it be a pleasant surprise once he shows up.

B: This is the best option. It is a quiet, personal, and cheap way of spending some time together.

6. A: This is a safe and romantic choice. Where else is better for the first kiss than the top of the Ferris wheel?

B: While this move shows your willingness to be brave for him, the last thing he wants to see is you turn green. Be careful if you feel timid about handling yourself.

7. A: You don't want your parents finding out you disobeyed their rules. One small breach might cause them to mistrust you, and the repercussions could be more severe.

B: Smoother move. Although you might feel childish and embarrassed to turn him down, in the long run, this is the safest bet!

ARE YOU MORE THAN A HOOKUP?

Do you want more than just a quick roll? Take this quiz to find out what has long-term potential and what's as fleeting as a fresh manicure.

■ ■

1 **You've hooked up three weekends in a row—but he has yet to offer any notion of boyfriend/girlfriend. When you bring it up, he**

___**a.** says he's too busy with lacrosse to be your boyfriend.

X **b.** says, "I assumed we were together."

___**c.** says, "I'm already dating Jane. Didn't you know?"

2 **After a steamy hookup session, your man**

X **a.** holds you tight for a posthookup cuddle session.

___**b.** ducks out—he's meeting the guys for tacos in fifteen minutes.

___**c.** offers to drive you home.

3 When you hang out for an hour at your house on Friday night, you spend how much time hooking up?

__**a.** The whole hour.

__**b.** Half an hour.

✗**c.** Twenty minutes.

♥ ♥ ♥

4 His friend's nickname for you is

__**a.** Easy Mary.

__**b.** Rambunctious Rachel.

✗**c.** Princess Pam.

♥ ♥ ♥

5 After a hookup with your man, you would guess that tomorrow in class he'll

✗**a.** sit next to you and smile.

__**b.** walk by wearing sunglasses.

__**c.** call in sick.

SCORING

Give yourself the following points for each answer, then add up your total:

1. A-2   B-3   C-1
2. A-3   B-1   C-2
3. A-1   B-2   C-3
4. A-1   B-2   C-3
5. A-3   B-2   C-1

mommy

13–15 Points: LONG-TERM POTENTIAL

This guys shows he's into you for more than just a night of passion. His assumption you were already an item is a good indication. While the two of you might spend a chunk of the night hooking up, he is clearly interested in more than the physical bonuses. Especially if the day after the hookup he sat next to you and smiled, it is obvious he digs you.

9–12 Points: WORTHWHILE, MAYBE

It may be too soon to tell if this guy is interested in more than the initial physical fever. Offering to drive you home after a hookup either could be an indication he has other plans afterward or could show his interest in your safety. If his excuse is that he's too busy for a girlfriend, but wants to keep hooking up, leave him behind.

5-8 Points: BOOTY

If your guy scores here, you should can him and walk away before you get emotionally attached. If he ditches you after a hookup to meet the guys for tacos, he is not worth your time. The fact that this player already has a girlfriend proves his interest lies only in physical passion. Also, his infidelity should make it clear that you're much too good for him.

What Kind of a
GIRLFRIEND Are You?

Are you a hopeless romantic—or are you lusty and proud of it? Take this quiz to find out just what type of girlfriend you are.

■■■■■■■■■■■■■■■■■■■■■■■■■■■■■■■■

1 **When your honey is sick, you**

__**a.** rush over with his favorite movies and soup.

__**b.** Steer clear—you don't want any of his germs.

✗**c.** make him a special homemade card and hand-deliver it with flowers.

2 **At his games you show up**

✗**a.** while they warm up—you don't want to miss a second.

__**b.** in time for the after-game wrap-up meeting and tailgate party.

__**c.** at halftime—you were busy setting up a romantic dinner.

3 **In class, you slide him a note that says:**

~~**a.**~~ "How did I get so lucky?"

__**b.** "I want you, I need you."

__**c.** "I love you."

♥ ♥ ♥

4 **After school, the two of you head**

__**a.** to your house to finish homework—that way, you can spend the weekend together without work hanging over your head.

__**b.** to your bedroom—you haven't kissed since lunch.

~~**c.**~~ out for a walk—you can't wait to hold his hand and get a big hug.

♥ ♥ ♥

5 **You typically go to**

~~**a.**~~ fun movies—you both love to laugh the whole way through.

__**b.** any movie—from the back row, it is hard to tell which one is playing.

__**c.** whatever movie is out—as long as you are together, it doesn't matter what's playing.

6 **On a Sunday afternoon, you'd rather**

___**a.** shoot some hoops.

___**b.** make out.

✗**c.** cuddle listening to music.

7 **In the yearbook, you were voted**

✗**a.** cutest couple.

___**b.** most "hands on" couple.

___**c.** most in love.

8 **You met him**

✗**a.** in the nurse's office.

___**b.** playing "truth or dare."

___**c.** at a poetry reading.

9 **You prefer to receive**

X **a.** a warm hug.

___ **b.** a pound of gummy-worms.

___ **c.** flowers, flowers, flowers.

♥ ♥ ♥

10 **For your one-year anniversary, he**

X **a.** took you where you first met for a picnic.

___ **b.** bought you lingerie.

___ **c.** dedicated your song on the radio and showed up at your door to take you to dinner.

ANSWERS

Mostly A's: BOY'S BEST FRIEND

You're like two peas in a pod. He knows what you love and doesn't hold back showing you he cares. You support him in everything he does and you find time to spend with him during the busiest of times. The two of you are a great match and enjoy the simpler pleasures like a picnic or hugs. He knows already what a great catch you are.

Mostly B's: LUSTFUL LOVER

You're crazy about each other and your obvious physical attraction can hardly be hidden. But take time to know more than just his chemical reactions. Go on a walk, bowling, or to the batting cages. Being outside together can be a fun, entertaining time, too.

Mostly C's: GIRLY GIRLFRIEND

You're a true romantic, lapping up the flowers, love songs, and serenades. Sensitive guys who please you will win your heart. It is clear you are wild for this type—remember to take time to be together, whether it be for a movie or a walk.

do you **always fall** for the **bad boys?**

While there's always been a special place in our hearts for bad boys of the music and movie world, in real life, it's way different. Unless you dig being made unhappy, you may want to learn how to avoid these fools. Take this quiz to see what you really think about the wrong guys.

■■■■■■■■■■■■■■■■■■■■■■■■■■■■■■■

Check yes or no:

	YES	NO
1 When you get in a fight with your boyfriend, are you scared he will break up with you?		
2 Has he forgotten more than one anniversary date?		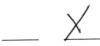
3 Has he ever belittled you to make himself feel more powerful?		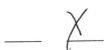

	YES	NO
4 Has he ever ganged up on you with his pals to get a good laugh?	___	X
5 Have you ever felt embarrassed in public by the way he treats you?	___	X
6 Does he say he'll stop by but doesn't show up?	___	X
7 Has he ever promised to call and "forgot"?	___	X
8 Do you ever feel like he is sneaking around behind your back?	___	X
9 Do you feel like he plays mind games?	X	___
10 Has he ever cheated on you?	___	X
11 Is he known as a "player"?	___	X
12 Does he cancel your plans at the last minute?	___	X

YES   NO

13 Does he ever show up at your games to support you? — X | —

14 Do you feel manipulated by him? — | X

15 Is he domineering, often making you feel inferior to him? — | X

16 At a restaurant, does he eat off your plate, too—without asking you first? — | X

17 Do your friends think he is a control freak? — | X

ANSWERS

If you answered yes to more than ten of these questions, then take a minute to think about the guys you date—and yourself. No one should be with a guy who embarrasses her in public or cheats on her. If he acts domineering and tends to break up with you after silly fights, perhaps it's time to focus your interests on another type of guy. Especially if your friends think he is a player or sneaking around behind your back, trust their instincts and be careful—you might be getting played by a bad boy.

AREYOU**STALKING**HIM?

Sure, every girl secretly wants to scope out her crush 24/7, but sometimes Sherlocking can turn weird if it's too 'xtreme. See if your radar style is sane or way sorry by checking the answers you most agree with:

1 You've memorized not only his daily schedule but those of his sibs and parents, too.

☒ Sometimes ❑ A Lot ❑ What's Wrong with That?

2 Drive-bys are a part of your A.M. and P.M. routines.

☒ Sometimes ❑ A Lot ❑ What's Wrong with That?

3 Purse-size binoculars look good to you.

☒ Sometimes ❑ A Lot ❑ What's Wrong with That?

4 You schedule your study hall and lunch periods to spy on him.

☒ Sometimes ❑ A Lot ❑ What's Wrong with That?

5 At night you mull over every detail of the day's spottings and encounters.

❑ Sometimes ☒ A Lot ❑ What's Wrong with That?

6 You show up at every public function he attends.

☒ Sometimes ❑ A Lot ❑ What's Wrong with That?

7 Encounters with his sibs give you a chance to pry for exciting information.

☒ Sometimes ❑ A Lot ❑ What's Wrong with That?

8 Walking the dog by his house has become your new hobby.

☒ Sometimes ❑ A Lot ❑ What's Wrong with That?

9 You're becoming very interested in digging up info on his past crushes.

☒ Sometimes ❑ A Lot ❑ What's Wrong with That?

10 You practice different ways of saying hello when you "accidentally" bump into him.

☒ Sometimes ❑ A Lot ❑ What's Wrong with That?

11 It's more fun to think about him than to see him.

☒ Sometimes ❑ A Lot ❑ What's Wrong with That?

12 You manage to worm your way into his favorite clubs.

☒ Sometimes ❑ A Lot ❑ What's Wrong with That?

13 You follow him to dark movie theaters, where you can do some of your best surveillance work.

☒ Sometimes ❑ A Lot ❑ What's Wrong with That?

SCORING

1–5 "Sometimes": WITHIN NORMAL LIMITS

We all wonder what our crush is up to—but we don't act on off-the-wall impulses.

3–5 "A Lot": APPROACHING DANGER

A little more reality would be best here. Try going without thinking of him for two weeks.

6+ "What's Wrong with That?": DERANGED SPY CHICK

Abort mission! Danger Zone

You need to come into the sunlight and get a guy who's really in your life—not just your head. Remember, it takes two to make a couple.

chapter TWO
BOYFRIENDS

Boyfriend dilemmas come in all different guises. You could fall hard and heavy for a summer hottie only to have to separate come fall. Or you could waste lots of time trying to figure out why a guy who says he likes you drools over every girl he passes. The truth is that when it comes to boyfriends, there really is no smooth course. This chapter is devoted to these guys whom we love and hate—depending on how they behave. We invite you along as we take a good hard look at the stuff that's involved in having a beau—from bogus to cool.

is a **boyfriend** a **total** necessity?

Are you attached to your guy or are you an independent woman? Do you need him 24/7 or do you lean on your gal pals for support? Take this quiz to find out whether you can cope with—or without—your boyfriend.

1 How much time do you spend primping before a night out?

__**a.** Less than half an hour.

__**b.** More than forty minutes.

__**c.** More than an hour and a half.

2 While on-line, you talk mostly to

__**a.** your girlfriends.

__**b.** your guy.

__**c.** anyone who is on-line but mostly the friends from your buddy list.

3 **Around the holidays, you feel most stressed over**

___**a.** what to get your guy.

___**b.** gifts—what are you going to make for your friends?

___**c.** stress—these are the holidays!

4 **You're more concerned with what**

___**a.** he thinks.

___**b.** your friends think.

___**c.** no one thinks.

5 **At the dance, you'd rather be with**

___**a.** a group of friends, both guys and girls.

___**b.** just your man.

___**c.** the girls for a night of fun times.

6 **Your coach says your jump shot needs work. You**

___**a.** call your guy for tips.

___**b.** invite over the girls for a game of hoops.

___**c.** work on it by yourself in the gym.

7 **You're heartbroken over a failed midterm. You**

___ **a.** call the girls for an emergency sob session.

___ **b.** drive straight to your boyfriend's to lean on his shoulder.

✗ **c.** walk it off alone.

8 **The new flick is out and you're dying to go. You would cancel for**

___ **a.** nothing—you've been waiting months.

✗ **b.** your best friend's spur-of-the-moment breakup.

___ **c.** your guy's lame gig at the local mall.

9 **Do you shop**

___ **a.** with him?

✗ **b.** alone?

___ **c.** with the girls?

10 **Your dream day is spent**

___ **a.** alone, peaceful and serene.

___ **b.** with him by yourselves.

✗ **c.** out with your buds.

SCORING

Give yourself the following points for each answer,
then add up your total:

1. A-1   B-2   C-3
2. A-1   B-3   C-2
3. A-3   B-2   C-1
4. A-3   B-2   C-1
5. A-1   B-3   C-2
6. A-3   B-2   C-1
7. A-2   B-3   C-1
8. A-1   B-2   C-3
9. A-3   B-1   C-2
10. A-1   B-3   C-2

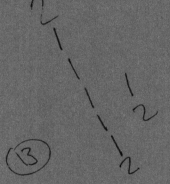

10–16 Points: INDEPENDENT WOMAN

You excel at balancing girlfriends and your special
guy. Most importantly, you take time for yourself.
You'd rather escape alone to shop or to do the
things you've been wanting to do—whether it's
that special movie or that trip you've wanted to
take. This shows a great sense of self-worth and
confidence.

17–22 Points: BALANCED BABE

You're pretty good at keeping both your guy and your girlfriends in your life. Occasionally, you'll take time to be alone for a quiet afternoon. You'd compromise your plans to help others who need your shoulder to cry on or simply a ride home. This shows a great willingness to put others before yourself.

23–30 Points: LIFE SUPPORT

You depend on your guy to be your shoulder to lean on, your support at school, and your party-time partner. This means the two of you share a great comfort level and you feel you can rely on him in tough times. Try spending some time with your girls more often—they may feel left out. And don't forget to take time for yourself, too. You don't want to leave the most important person out!

How Do You Know If It's **FOR REAL?**

He may be your first boy—or the latest in a long line. Whatever. With boyfriends and romance—just like food—it's important to know what's good for you and what's merely empty calories. Feast your eyes below to see how good a judge you are of the real thing.

■■■■■■■■■■■■■■■■■■■■■■■■■■■■■■■■

Check what feels right to you:

YES   NO

1 He likes talking to you.

2 He cancels plans with his buds to be with you.

3 When he met your family, he was nervous.

4 He's always "busy" on gift-exchanging occasions, like birthdays and Valentine's Day.

	YES	NO
5 You have a shared vocabulary.	X	—
6 You know each other's middle names.	X	—
7 The most affectionate thing he calls you is "kiddo."	—	X
8 If you're cold, he tells you to pull down your sleeves.	—	X
9 He wants you to sit next to him in public.	X	—
10 He can order your favorite foods for you.	—	X
11 Chronically late is his style.	—	X
12 He doesn't call you until a couple of days after returning from a vacation.	—	X
13 He "forgets" when you have a doctor's appointment.	X	—

SCORING

If you answered

1. Yes—it's real.
2. Yes—it's real.
3. Yes—it's real.
4. No—it's romance lite.
5. Yes—it's real.
6. Yes—it's real.
7. No—it's romance lite.

8. No—it's romance lite.
9. Yes—it's real.
10. Yes—it's real.
11. No—it's romance lite.
12. No—it's romance lite.
13. No—it's romance lite.

Mostly Yes:

You have a highly developed sense of romance. You know how to treat others well and be treated well yourself in return.

Middle Ground: ✓

You're probably very trusting of your guy—or maybe you're just playing with him until the real thing comes along.

Mostly No:

Take out those rose-colored contacts, girl! Your idea of romance is about as heavy as a skim milk latte and just as nourishing. Go for the real thing.

is your guy
TOO FAST
or **TOO** SLOW?

Are you spending your time speeding down the fast lane or are you putt-putting into reverse? Take this quiz to find out if your plan is moving at the right pace.

1 You feel satisfied with your relationship.
☑ YES ☐ NO

2 He's always begging for more.
☐ YES ☑ NO

3 You feel pressured to go further.
☐ YES ☑ NO

4 You wish he'd step it up a notch.
☐ YES ☑ NO

5 His idea of a wild night is *Robocop 2*.
☐ YES ☑ NO

6 You waited more than a month to hit second base.
☑ YES ☐ NO

7 He's suggesting things you've never heard of.
☐ YES ☑ NO

8 His long list of prior hookups intimidates you.
☑ YES ☐ NO

9 Everything is going at a comfortable pace.
☑ YES ☐ NO

10 How do you like it? More, more, more?
☐ YES ☑ NO

ANSWERS

3+ YES

You often feel pressured to go further than you may otherwise feel comfortable. It might be because of his experience or you may just prefer to take it slow. Talk to him before things go too far. Communicating with him about your concerns will eliminate sticky situations later.

3+ NO

Putt-putting along the freeway is no fun. You wish he'd step it up a bit and turn up the heat. Knock him into action by suggesting you turn off the movie and listen to music. If he's inexperienced, understand he is probably nervous and talk to him about taking the next step. If this doesn't get you anywhere, face it, he's a washout.

Equal Mix of YES and NO

You are at a great place with your guy and are satisfied with your relationship's progress. It's okay to feel "off pace" once in a while but never to feel pressured. Keep up the good work and be sure to talk to him if you get off track.

Is an **older guy** **RIGHT** FOR YOU?

The older guys do have experience—but maybe they want more than you're prepared to give. Let's see how you feel about the "age issue" with this quiz.

■ ■

1 What do you consider an older guy?

__**a.** One to two years older.

__**b.** Two to three years older.

✗**c.** Four years–plus.

2 How would your parents view anyone more than four years older than you?

__**a.** They won't know—you lied about his age.

✗**b.** Weird.

__**c.** Senior citizen.

3 **If you were crushing on a much older guy and discovered that he was always attracted to younger girls, you would**

__**a.** revise your opinion downward about him.

__**b.** shrug it off.

__**c.** shrug him off.

4 **If he drives, what does that mean to you?**

__**a.** Not relying on Mom.

__**b.** Status.

__**c.** Four-wheeling whenever.

5 **Who are your friends more comfortable with?**

__**a.** Older guys.

__**b.** Guys their own age.

__**c.** Guys with IDs.

6 **Whom would you have more to talk about with?**

__ **a.** An older guy.

✗ **b.** A guy your age.

__ **c.** Anyone who can get into R movies.

♥ ♥ ♥

7 **You would describe your favorite actor as**

__ **a.** Harrison Ford.

__ **b.** Brad Pitt.

✗ **c.** Chris Klein.

♥ ♥ ♥

8 **Does your older guy want you to stay out late on school nights?**

__ **a.** Yes.

__ **b.** Occasionally.

✗ **c.** He goes without you.

9 How would you describe your image with an older guy?

__**a.** Cool.

__**b.** More mature than your friends.

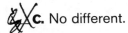**c.** No different.

10 Do you feel funny doing silly "young" things in front of him—like holding your favorite stuffed toy or special blanket?

__**a.** No, that's who you are.

X**b.** You did at first.

__**c.** Yes, he calls you a baby.

ANSWERS

	In Normal Range	Middling	Too Old!
1.	A	B	C
2.	C	B	A
3.	A	B	C
4.	A	B	C
5.	A	B	C
6.	A	B	C
7.	C	B	A
8.	C	B	A
9.	C	A	B
10.	A	B	C

MIND GAMES:
Is Your Crush **PLAYING** You?

Is he playing you like a bass guitar in his garage band? Take this quiz to determine who's the MVP and who's strictly bush league.

■ ■

1 **When your guy says he'll call at eight P.M., the phone rings at**

__**a.** ten P.M.

__**b.** eight P.M. sharp.

__**c.** What ring? He doesn't call.

2 **When your man calls to say he'll swing by after practice, he**

__**a.** stops by for a second but doesn't come in.

__**b.** shows up and stays for a while asking how your day was.

__**c.** beeps as he passes on his way home.

3 **When you are supposed to meet for the movies Friday, he**

__**a.** calls and says he can' t make it. How about Saturday?

☒**b.** meets you outside with the tickets.

__**c.** shows up with a bunch of his buddies.

4 **After a hot and heavy hookup, your man says:**

__**a.** "Was that good or what?"

☒**b.** "Was everything okay for you?"

__**c.** "Do we have to stop?"

5 **The day after your first hookup, he**

__**a.** says hi but doesn't stop to chat.

☒**b.** asks how you are and if you want to get together again.

__**c.** walks by you with his head down.

6 As you walk out of your fave store, you see your crush and his friends walking in your direction. He's laughing and joking around. When his eyes meet yours, he

__**a.** smiles.

b. comes over and introduces you to his pals.

__**c.** looks embarrassed that his friends might have seen him looking at you.

♥ ♥ ♥

7 At a party Saturday night, your man spends how much time with you?

__**a.** Half an hour.

b. All night.

__**c.** No time at all.

♥ ♥ ♥

8 When you talk to your man, his hands are usually

__**a.** around your shoulder.

b. around your waist.

__**c.** all over you.

9 **When you are together in public, do you feel like your personal space is invaded?**

__**a.** Sometimes.

X**b.** Never.

__**c.** Always.

♥ ♥ ♥

10 **When the end-of-the-year dance is coming up, you cross your fingers that your crush will ask you. As the date approaches, he asks**

__**a.** a week in advance.

X**b.** three weeks in advance.

__**c.** the night before.

SCORING

Mostly A's: MINOR LEAGUE

While your man is showing positive signs he's into you, this might not be the real deal. He is steering clear of mind games, which is a great sign, but be careful: His inability to be punctual and keep his word may prove he is not being straightforward with you.

Mostly B's: ALL-STAR

This guy is wild about you and it shows. He stops by when he says he will, and keeping his word is a true sign of wanting to be with you. His body language is also indicative of his true feelings. Stick with this guy—he could be a great catch.

Mostly C's: HE'S OUT

That's it! This guy has had more than three strikes. His inconsistency is a true sign he might be playing you for his benefit. His level of carelessness borders on the rude. Beware of this guy, he could be the master player!

is he *INSANELY* JEALOUS?

A drop of jealousy can be healthy and add spice to a romance, but too much can make you sick. Measure his jealousy blood pressure with this quiz—to see if he's ready to burst a vessel or within normal limits.

■ ■

1 **When another guy tells you you look hot, he**

__**a.** grins.

__**b.** growls.

__**c.** simmers all night.

♥ ♥ ♥

2 **If he finds you flirting with a hunky guy, he says:**

__**a.** "Later for you!"

__**b.** "Let's dance."

__**c.** "You'll pay."

3 **The last time you wore that sports bra, he**

__**a.** covered you with his varsity jacket.

X **b.** stared all night.

__**c.** said you looked trashy.

♥ ♥ ♥

4 **He learns the guy you used to crush on has called you. He**

X **a.** pretends it's okay.

__**b.** warns the guy off.

__**c.** stops calling you.

♥ ♥ ♥

5 **While in the mall, two young guys whistle at you. He**

X **a.** tells them to bug off.

__**b.** glares.

__**c.** makes like it's your fault.

6 **If he could pick out your shoes, they would be**

X **a.** stiletto sandals.

__ **b.** gym shoes.

__ **c.** flats.

♥ ♥ ♥

7 **When he learned you baked your old beau a big batch of birthday cookies, he**

__ **a.** blew like a volcano.

__ **b.** tossed his own cookies.

X **c.** vowed to treat you better.

♥ ♥ ♥

8 **When reading your yearbook, he came across some passionate autographs. He**

__ **a.** crossed them out.

X **b.** read them with interest.

__ **c.** wrote some of his own—even steamier!

9 When you tell him you are going to the mall with your buds, do you spot him spying from behind the food court?

__**a.** Wrong guy.

__**b.** Maybe you are dreaming.

__**c.** . . . And by the Gap and J. Crew.

♥ ♥ ♥

10 Does he snoop in your locker?

__**a.** Never.

__**b.** Only for something he "left there."

__**c.** Every day.

ANSWERS

Give yourself the following points for each answer:

1. A-1   B-2   C-3
2. A-2   B-1   C-3
3. A-2   B-1   C-3
4. A-1   B-2   C-3
5. A-1   B-2   C-3
6. A-1   B-2   C-3
7. A-1   B-2   C-3
8. A-1   B-2   C-3
9. A-1   B-2   C-3
10. A-1   B-2   C-3

Mostly 1's and a Sprinkling of 2's

His jealousy is normal, maybe even a little cute!

More 2's Than 1's

Could mean trouble. If he goes from ridiculous to raging, lose him.

Lots of 2's and 3's

This guy is as changeable as a werewolf and about as sensitive. Find someone who's in control of himself before he drags you down.

should you STAY FRIENDS after THE BREAKUP?

A girl faces many postsplit decisions—like, "Do I need a new hairstyle?"—but one that deserves extra-careful consideration is how to treat the ex-main squeeze. Even if the breakup wasn't one you sought, there are ways to minimize hurt feelings while increasing your coolness. Review the situations below to see how you would handle yourself.

■ ■

On a scale of 1 to 5, how important is it to

	1	**2**	**3**	**4**	**5**
1 run into him soon so tension doesn't build up?	1	2	③	4	5
2 erase his number from your speed dial?	1	2	3	4	⑤
3 clean out your locker shrine to him?	1	2	3	4	⑤

	1	**2**	**3**	**4**	**5**

4 tell your friends about the breakup?
1 2 3 (4) 5

5 remain cordial with his buds?
(1) 2 3 4 5

6 act like nothing disastrous happened?
1 (2) 3 4 5

7 bad-mouth him behind his back?
(1) 2 3 4 5

8 flirt like crazy with his buds?
(1) 2 3 4 5

9 drop out of any clubs you were in together?
1 (2) 3 4 5

10 act syrupy when you see him?
(1) 2 3 4 5

11 stop thinking of yourself as "damaged goods"?
1 (2) 3 4 5

12 stop talking about him?
1 2 (3) 4 5

13 make up a wicked nickname for him?
1 (2) 3 4 5

1 2 3 4 5

14 act indifferent when
you learn he has a new love? (1) 2 3 4 5

15 still give him birthday
cards and stuff? (1) 2 3 4 5

16 find ways to run
into him? (1) 2 3 4 5

17 keep in touch with
his family? (1) 2 3 4 5

18 be friends with his
new love? 1 2 (3) 4 5

19 return his gifts? (1) 2 3 4 5

20 set him up with
your friends? (1) 2 3 4 5

SCORING

Here's how we see it:

1. If you checked 4 or 5, you're not letting bad feelings build up. You've got to see him sometime—make it sooner.

2. Again, 4 or 5 is the most realistic answer.

3. Anywhere from 3 up means you're moving on.

4. 4 or 5: Sharing your wounded feelings with good buds will help you heal faster.

5. Remaining friends with his buds takes willpower, so 5 is the best answer. You don't have to be permanently in their lives, you can always ease out.

6. Acting like you can handle the breakup merits a 3 or more.

7. Bad-mouthing is tricky—if it backfires, you look bad. We give this a 1.

8. 1: Flirting with his buds won't get you far.

9. 1: You can't always avoid him—and after a while it will get stale.

10. 1 or 2: Don't be phony—you could look psycho.

11. Never think of yourself as a loser. This rates a 5.

12. 1 to 3: After a while, you may have no reason to.

13. 1: Making up nicknames could be fun at first, but drop it fast even if it's only in your own head. You deserve better.

14. 4 or 5: Don't follow his every move as though it's topic number one in your life.

15. 3 or less: Only give him totally innocent friend-type gifts, then taper off as you build up a new love.

16. Running into him isn't going to work. Score a 1.

17. Staying in touch with his family is cute, but eventually he'll have a new girl and you'll start to look dorky. It's a 3.

18. This is a 2. You could accidentally bare your fangs with his new love, and then you'll look bad!

19. Returning his gifts is a 4 or 5. Let go!

20. Matchmaking with your friends? Wait a while!

If most of your answers agreed with ours, then you're *strong* and *healthy*. Keeping old crushes light not only makes you look good, but leaves you ready for another.

If your answers strongly disagreed with ours, maybe you want to rethink what's good for you after a breakup. Sure, we all need time to recharge, but carrying on like a "wronged woman" makes things much worse. Look ahead with optimism to the next crush and meantime get out and roll with your buds. There will be lots more romance for you.

DOES HE KEEP
YOU WAITING?

You've started your love engines and Romeo is nowhere in sight. What's a reasonable excuse and what's AWOL? Take a look below at typical scenarios and decide how you would rate them if they happened to you.

■■■■■■■■■■■■■■■■■■■■■■■■■■■■■■■

Check off your call:

1 He calls from his weekend job to say he's running late.

☒ Give Him a Pass   ☐ Think Twice   ☐ No Way

2 He said he'd be by "later." That was over five hours ago.

☐ Give Him a Pass   ☒ Think Twice   ☐ No Way

3 Your birthday present was ordered "over a month ago." Really!

☐ Give Him a Pass   ☒ Think Twice   ☐ No Way

4 "Watches are for everybody else," he says.

❏ Give Him a Pass ❏ Think Twice ☒ No Way

5 You both need extra study time for the finals, so at the last minute, he suggests canceling plans.

☒ Give Him a Pass ❏ Think Twice ❏ No Way

6 He "forgets" to come by, then says he called but your line was busy.

☒ Give Him a Pass ❏ Think Twice ❏ No Way

7 He tells you his game may run late.

☒ Give Him a Pass ❏ Think Twice ❏ No Way

8 There's always a lot of confusion about appointments with him—but it's never his fault.

❏ Give Him a Pass ☒ Think Twice ❏ No Way

9 It's a week before Homecoming and he hasn't confirmed plans for the dance.

❏ Give Him a Pass ☒ Think Twice ❏ No Way

10 "Something" comes up with his buds a lot.

❏ Give Him a Pass   ☒ Think Twice   ❏ No Way

11 His answering machine is always on.

❏ Give Him a Pass   ☒ Think Twice   ❏ No Way

12 He's an electronics whiz, so you asked him to help set up your new CD player—that was last month.

❏ Give Him a Pass   ☒ Think Twice   ❏ No Way

13 He went into the deli for a soda and left you waiting for a half hour.

❏ Give Him a Pass   ☒ Think Twice   ❏ No Way

14 "I'm so sorry" are his first words if he's late.

❏ Give Him a Pass   ☒ Think Twice   ❏ No Way

15 He borrowed your favorite CD—last summer!

❏ Give Him a Pass   ❏ Think Twice   ☒ No Way

ANSWERS

1. A ✓   6. C ✗   11. B ✓
2. B ✓   7. A ✓   12. B ✓
3. C ✗ ✓   8. B ✓ ✓   13. C ✗
4. C ✓   9. B ✓   14. A ✗ ✓
5. A ✓   10. C ✗   15. C ✓

Mostly Right: TIME IS ON YOUR SIDE, TEEN

You know the real score.

Midrange: TIME IS ON YOUR HANDS

You might want to put those wasted hours to work for you—try keeping *him* waiting for a change. Things might improve.

Way Off: A DAY LATE AND A DOLLAR SHORT

There's nothing cool about your coming in last—or being too forgiving. Get rid of this fool fast as a New York minute.

can you make it work
LONG DISTANCE?

You met him at camp or your family's vacation house—or he's moved away. Your love is too intense to break off. What's left to you is something telephone companies love—long-distance romance. Take this quiz to find out if you're prepared to cope with the geographical divide and the strains of maintaining closeness while being far apart.

■ ■

1 **Typically you send _____ letters a week to your man.**

__**a.** 3–4

X **b.** 1–2

__**c.** 0

2 **You have enough time to send _____ e-mails a day.**

X **a.** 4+

X **b.** 2–3

__**c.** maybe 1

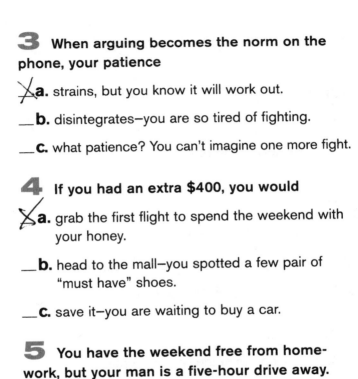

3 **When arguing becomes the norm on the phone, your patience**

☒**a.** strains, but you know it will work out.

__**b.** disintegrates—you are so tired of fighting.

__**c.** what patience? You can't imagine one more fight.

4 **If you had an extra $400, you would**

☒**a.** grab the first flight to spend the weekend with your honey.

__**b.** head to the mall—you spotted a few pair of "must have" shoes.

__**c.** save it—you are waiting to buy a car.

5 **You have the weekend free from homework, but your man is a five-hour drive away. After school Friday, you**

__**a.** hit the road—you want to be there ASAP.

☒**b.** wait until Saturday morning, then get up early to see your love.

__**c.** stay home—five hours is way too long to drive for the weekend.

6 **On your list of priorities, he is**

__ **a.** numero uno.

__ **b.** below school, work, and friends.

__ **c.** bottom of the totem pole.

7 **Is he worth the effort?**

__ **a.** Absolutely.

__ **b.** Most of the time.

__ **c.** When you aren't fighting.

8 **He's supposed to call at ten P.M. You**

__ **a.** get home at nine-thirty, just in case he calls early.

__ **b.** rush home at ten hoping not to miss the call.

__ **c.** get caught up at the library. Oops!

9 **When he isn't there, you feel**

__ **a.** hopelessly lonely and incomplete.

__ **b.** sad and lonely once in a while.

__ **c.** free—no one to watch you all the time.

10 Whenever you meet someone with the same name as his, you instantly think:

___**a.** "Oh, cute! I miss him so much."

___**b.** "Gosh, it is tough being apart."

___**c.** "Funny, how small the world is."

11 While cruising with friends, you hear your "couple" song on the radio. You

___**a.** hush everyone down so you can hear every word.

___**b.** listen by yourself.

___**c.** change the station—they'll think you're silly.

12 While shopping at the mall, you see something you know he would love. You

___**a.** bake him his favorite cookies instead and send him a surprise package in the morning.

___**b.** package it up and send it out later in the week.

___**c.** pass it up—next time maybe.

13 You send his letters

___**a.** all decked out with stickers and cartoons.

___**b.** with cute stamps.

___**c.** in plain envelopes.

14 At a party Friday night, your former flutter flirts with you. Are you tempted?

a. Never. You know where your heart is.

b. Maybe. You miss your guy so much, but he is far away and your ex is near.

c. But it's so hard to be faithful.

15 He's a thousand miles away. Do you trust him?

a. Always. You know he is loyal.

b. Most of the time.

c. It's hard to say. There must be other girls who he is interested in.

16 You set up strict rules for hanging out with other guys. Are you true to your rules?

a. Of course. It is natural for you to hang out with other guys as long as you stay true to your man.

b. Most of the time, but when the cute ones call, who knows?

c. Rules, what rules? When he is away, no one will know.

SCORING

Mostly A's: LONG-DISTANCE LOVER

You're ready for the commitment. You realize the stress of being far away but accept the compromises you'll have to make in order for your romance to work. Your commitment to him is worth your time and you take every chance to be with him, even for a weekend. Just don't let him take over your life. As much as you may love him, you have to be true to yourself first and foremost.

Mostly B's: SHORT-TERM SISTA

Be careful. You have to weigh your options and make sure this is what you really want. You seem to be on the fence about staying loyal. Are you ready for the sacrifice it will take to make this relationship work? While the short term may be smooth, in the long run, your lonely heart might chase you into someone else's arms.

Mostly C's: HOMEBODY

Being away from your sweetie is a drag and it is clear you aren't ready for the time and effort it will take to be a real girlfriend. Your eyes tend to wander and you're getting tired of fighting and lose patience easily. You need your man to be close and with you most of the time.

ARE YOU "JUST FRIENDS"?

When does a guy go from being someone you hang with to your would-be lover? There are signals. Suddenly the bud you used to skateboard with looks as hot as Jude Law (or so you think!). If your heart jump-starts when you hear his name, it may be time to create a new folder for your friendship—one called love.

To find out how crush-worthy your pal may be, take this quiz.

■ ■

Check one answer:

1 When he calls, the family says, "Uh-oh."
- ☒ New Things You Notice
- ❏ Always Been Like That
- ☒ Not Really

2 You're amazed at what a great sense of humor he has.
- ☒ New Things You Notice
- ☒ Always Been Like That
- ❏ Not Really

3 Your chats have a flirty edge.

☒ New Things You Notice
❑ Always Been Like That
❑ Not Really

4 You don't think his girlfriends are ever good enough for him.

❑ New Things You Notice
☒ Always Been Like That
❑ Not Really

5 You'd want to be stranded on a desert island with him.

☒ New Things You Notice
❑ Always Been Like That
❑ Not Really

6 Lately, you don't enjoy telling him about your other crushes.

☒ New Things You Notice
❑ Always Been Like That
❑ Not Really

7 He teases you more.

☒ New Things You Notice
❑ Always Been Like That
❑ Not Really

8 Instead of Pacey from *Dawson's Creek*, his face pops into your head at bedtime.

☒ New Things You Notice
❑ Always Been Like That
❑ Not Really

9 When he puts his arm around you, it feels great.

☒ New Things You Notice
❑ Always Been Like That
❑ Not Really

10 The two of you enjoy doing nothing.

☒ New Things You Notice
❑ Always Been Like That
❑ Not Really

11 When did he start to look so hunky?

- ☑ New Things You Notice
- ❑ Always Been Like That
- ❑ Not Really

12 When you had to work late together on a tough school project, time flew by.

- ☑ New Things You Notice
- ❑ Always Been Like That
- ❑ Not Really

13 You're on-line buddies.

- ☑ New Things You Notice
- ❑ Always Been Like That
- ❑ Not Really

14 On the last school trip, he sat next to you on the bus.

- ☑ New Things You Notice
- ❑ Always Been Like That
- ❑ Not Really

15 You think about everything he says to you.

- ☑ New Things You Notice
- ❑ Always Been Like That
- ❑ Not Really

16 He has fabulous eyelashes.

- ☑ New Things You Notice
- ❑ Always Been Like That
- ❑ Not Really

17 The buzz is he likes you.

- ☑ New Things You Notice
- ❑ Always Been Like That
- ❑ Not Really

18 You spend more time passing his locker.

- ☑ New Things You Notice
- ❑ Always Been Like That
- ❑ Not Really

19 His name is doodled all over your telephone book.

- ☒ New Things You Notice
- ☐ Always Been Like That
- ☐ Not Really

20 You're flashing ahead to Valentine's Day.

- ☒ New Things You Notice
- ☐ Always Been Like That
- ☐ Not Really

21 You got the recipe for his favorite cookies

- ☒ New Things You Notice
- ☐ Always Been Like That
- ☒ Not Really

SCORING

Mostly "NOT REALLY"

Relax, your temperature is not on the rise. You're just friends.

Mostly "ALWAYS BEEN LIKE THAT"

You're supergood friends, so good you could be in love and not know it.

Mostly "NEW THINGS YOU NOTICE"

This boy is certainly making a march on your heart. To make those love chimes ring even louder, try being alone with him—on a long walk, a trip to a museum—so you have time to explore this new region of romance.

WHAT DO YOUR
gifts TELL HIM?

Giving special things to your guy is wonderful. Guy gifts can be as romantic as one perfect flower or as spontaneous as a batch of freshly baked choc o'chips. But every gift comes with an invisible message—one that says something about the way the giver cares. Find out how good you are at the language of gifts with this quiz.

1 It's his birthday. He's always yearned for a puppy. You give him

__**a.** a ten-week-old golden retriever.

✗**b.** a cuddly stuffed animal.

__**c.** your family dog to baby-sit.

2 Valentine's Day, you'll make

__**a.** a photo album with head shots of you.

__**b.** a list of the things you want him to do for you.

✗**c.** a small handmade heart-shaped pillow with your initials.

3 **Fixing things is his passion. What's better than**

✗ **a.** a nifty toolbox?

___ **b.** your parents' broken appliances?

___ **c.** a book about antique Asian hand tools—written in Japanese?

4 **Food treats are a great way to his heart. You treat him to**

✗ **a.** a surprise party for two with all his faves.

___ **b.** a vegan meal.

___ **c.** your latest diet food.

5 **He has a secret soft spot for babies. Knowing that, you**

___ **a.** make him look at all your baby photos, then promise to copy "one" for him.

___ **b.** buy him a king-size pair of baby booties.

✗ **c.** arrange to visit your cousin's newborn so he can get in some cuddle time.

6 He made the team! How would you celebrate?

__**a.** Give him a framed photograph of him in uniform.

__**b.** buy him a copy of *The Bad News Bears* for "inspiration."

✗**c.** Buy yourself a team jacket.

7 He's often told you he'd rather have a root canal than a surprise party. But his best bud is planning one for him. What to do?

__**a.** Meet him at the party.

✗**b.** Tell his bud the thought is great, but not to do it.

__**c.** Arrange to bring your crush yourself—after all, you've got a hot new party outfit.

8 You know he's broke. But it's Christmas. What's the right thing to do?

✗**a.** Agree to exchange kisses and hugs.

__**b.** Rewrap "loser" gifts you received and give them to him.

__**c.** Give him a hefty gift certificate for Victoria's Secret.

9 His mom gave his old Beatles *Rubber Soul* album to the yearbook fund-raiser. You

___**a.** order another on eBay and have the bill sent to him.

___**b.** tell him he can listen to yours.

✗ **c.** try to buy it at the sale for him.

10 He loves handmade things. You give him

✗**a.** a hand-knit scarf in his favorite color.

___**b.** wool, needles, and a knitting booklet.

___**c.** your mother's old hand-knit Norwegian sweater.

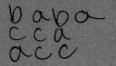

SCORING

SENSITIVE SOUL

If you scored mostly the answers below, your gifts tell him you're caring and thoughtful.

1. B	4. A	7. B	10. A
2. C	5. C	8. A	
3. A	6. A	9. C	

WACKY WOMAN

But if you chose mostly these answers below, you are so out there. Maybe your guy is, too—that's why you groove on each other.

1. A	4. B	7. A	10. B
2. B	5. B	8. B	
3. C	6. B	9. B	

EGO-TRIPPER

If your answers are heavy in this category, you're so into yourself, it's surprising you need a boyfriend. Change your me-first ways, or soon your crush will be changing you.

1. C	4. C	7. C	10. C
2. A	5. A	8. C	
3. B	6. C	9. A	

PDAs–HOW MUCH IS **TOO** MUCH?

Do you swap spit in the halls? Is it okay to play footsie under the table in class? Are there kids in school who turn any public space into their own not-so-private love clinic? Take this quiz to find out if you know if there are times when a Public Display of Affection is too much!

■■■■■■■■■■■■■■■■■■■■■■■■■■■■■

1 **You are in class with your Prince Charming. You sit in the back in order to**

__**a.** be near each other.

✗**b.** occasionally touch him with your foot or write a cute note on his book.

__**c.** grope his leg under the table.

2. **In the halls, you and your man**

✗**a.** walk next to each other.

__**b.** hold hands.

__**c.** make out.

3 **Time for the annual Homecoming bonfire!
You cuddle with your guy**

X **a.** on top of the blanket.

___**b.** half under.

___**c.** under up to your neck and hope there won't be
grass stains from rolling around.

♥ ♥ ♥

4 **At the spring formal, you and your date do
what on the dance floor?**

X **a.** Dance in a group.

___**b.** Slow dance.

___**c.** Bump and grind.

♥ ♥ ♥

5 **Is it ever okay to PDA in church or
synagogue?**

X **a.** Never

___**b.** Maybe

___**c.** Every time you go.

6 **At lunch you sit**

__**a.** across from him.

X **b.** next to him.

__**c.** on his lap.

7 **You're shopping together and you go in the dressing room to try something on. He**

__**a.** holds your shopping bags outside the store.

X **b.** waits to give you the thumbs-up.

__**c.** sneaks in for some lip locking.

8 **At the movies, you sit**

X **a.** in the middle row, in the center to get the best view.

__**b.** anywhere you can sit together and not get a neck cramp.

__**c.** in the back row, nice and private!

9 **At a party Saturday night, you two spend how much time "upstairs" together?**

___ **a.** There was an upstairs?

X **b.** Maybe twenty minutes.

___ **c.** There was a party downstairs?

10 **On the field-trip bus, you**

X **a.** sit with your friends, he with his.

X **b.** sit together.

___ **c.** share a seat and smooch the whole way.

SCORING

Mostly A's: SAFE . . . BUT SORRY?

While you like to save your affection for the private sphere, you could shake things up without getting embarrassing. Shyness a problem? Try sending him a cute note in class or cuddling at the night football game. You can always make some public areas more private than others.

Mostly B's: PERFECTLY PDA

You're super at sending him that "I'm crazy about you" signal, but never go overboard with your affection. You can easily find ways to show him you like him without grossing out those around you.

Mostly C's: GET A ROOM!

Think twice before groping each other. You may be making everyone around you feel uncomfortable. Be especially careful in such public spaces as church, where it is taboo for intense PDA. We suggest you tone it down a few notches.

DO YOU KNOW WHAT TO DO
after a fight?

Do you slam the door off its hinges—then come crawling back on your knees? Believe it or not, fighting is a form of communicating, and the way you behave after a fight can affect your relationship, too. So, don your referee's duds and see if you can call the best after-fight behavior.

■ ■

Check one answer:

1 If he doesn't understand why you're mad, you're not going to tell him!
❑ Healthy Winner ☒ Self-Defeating Loser

2 You're not going to let things go too long. That makes it harder to make up.
☒ Healthy Winner ❑ Self-Defeating Loser

3 Not speaking to him and not making eye contact gives you the upper hand.
❑ Healthy Winner ☒ Self-Defeating Loser

4 If you phone him and hang up several times, he'll get the message.

❏ Healthy Winner ☒ Self-Defeating Loser

5 It's good to say, "Let's both cool off, then talk."

☒ Healthy Winner ❏ Self-Defeating Loser

6 It's okay to apologize for things you didn't do.

❏ Healthy Winner ☒ Self-Defeating Loser

7 Feeling humiliated is just part of life.

☒ Healthy Winner ❏ Self-Defeating Loser

8 You'll call him and say you're sorry you disagreed and ask if you can meet.

☒ Healthy Winner ❏ Self-Defeating Loser

9 If he calls, you'll freeze him out.

❏ Healthy Winner ☒ Self-Defeating Loser

10 You'll tell all your friends what a jerk he is.

❏ Healthy Winner ☒ Self-Defeating Loser

11 Everything he ever gave you is history! You'll throw it on his lawn!

❏ Healthy Winner ☒ Self-Defeating Loser

12 You'll put a small bouquet of flowers in his locker.

☒ Healthy Winner ❏ Self-Defeating Loser

13 You'll write him a long bitter letter describing everything he's ever done wrong.

❏ Healthy Winner ☒ Self-Defeating Loser

14 After a good night's sleep, things will look better.

☒ Healthy Winner ❏ Self-Defeating Loser

15 Maybe you'll talk to him in a soft voice when you meet.

☒ Healthy Winner ❏ Self-Defeating Loser

16 You'll cut up all his love notes and throw them in his gym bag.

❏ Healthy Winner ☒ Self-Defeating Loser

17 When you do talk about the fight, you'll keep to the issues at hand.

☑ Healthy Winner ☒ Self-Defeating Loser

18 You'll think about what you could have done better.

☒ Healthy Winner ☐ Self-Defeating Loser

19 You'll tell him you expect a special present for making up.

☐ Healthy Winner ☒ Self-Defeating Loser

20 When you do make up, it's always so romantic. Almost worth fighting!

☒ Healthy Winner ☐ Self-Defeating Loser

ANSWERS

1. Self-defeating loser ✓
2. Healthy winner ✓
3. Self-defeating loser ✓
4. Self-defeating loser ✓
5. Healthy winner ✓
6. Self-defeating loser ✓
7. Self-defeating loser ✗
8. Healthy winner ✓
9. Self-defeating loser ✓
10. Self-defeating loser ✓
11. Self-defeating loser ✓
12. Healthy winner ✓
13. Self-defeating loser ✓
14. Healthy winner ✓
15. Healthy winner ✓
16. Self-defeating loser ✓
17. Healthy winner ✓
18. Healthy winner ✓
19. Self-defeating loser ✓
20. Healthy winner ✓

Mostly Right: MASTER PEACEMAKER

Relationships are not always smooth, but your responsible attitude will help smooth over the rough times. You're not above extending the olive branch or reaching out first.

Mostly Wrong: HIT and RUN

Impulsive behavior rarely feels good long term. Yes, you may feel a surge of triumph by trashing him or throwing away his gifts, but if you really like the guy, the only thing you're telling him is that you're dangerous and immature.

is your **BOYFRIEND** a **TERRIBLE FLIRT?**

Are his incessant come-on's a turn-off, or is this just normal teenage guy stuff? In other words, are his drooling and bug-eyed stare acceptable, or do they fall into the category of yucky, but what the hey? Take this test to determine what your attitudes are.

1 **How long can he go without coming on to a good-looking girl?**

___**a.** Less than one minute.

___**b.** Ten to fifteen minutes.

___**c.** Fifteen to thirty minutes.

2 **In an average day, about how many times would you get bummed out by his flirting?**

___**a.** Never.

___**b.** At least once.

___**c.** More than three times a day.

3 **Does he gawk at girls so much, you call him**

__**a.** Swivel Head?

__**b.** Babe?

__**c.** Mr. Former President?

♥ ♥ ♥

4 **You would describe your relationship as**

__**a.** very secure.

__**b.** mostly steady.

__**c.** minute to minute.

♥ ♥ ♥

5 **If you told him his flirting bothered you, what would he do?**

__**a.** Change his ways.

__**b.** Pick a fight.

__**c.** Change his girlfriend (you!).

6 **What would he do if you flirted openly in front of him?**

__**a.** Hm-mm-mmmm, good question.

__**b.** Ignore it.

__**c.** Take pointers.

♥ ♥ ♥

7 **How do you think you can make him stop?**

__**a.** By crying.

__**b.** By asking nicely.

__**c.** It's hopeless.

♥ ♥ ♥

8 **How does he act if a girl responds to his flirting in front of you?**

__**a.** Like the Road Runner.

__**b.** Like he's innocent.

__**c.** Very preoccupied.

9 How much do his come-ons bother you on a scale of 1 to 10?

__**a.** 8 to 10.

__**b.** 4 to 5.

__**c.** 1 to 3.

♥ ♥ ♥

10 Do you think he flirts because

__**a.** he wants to be liked?

__**b.** flirting runs in the family?

__**c.** he's looking for action?

♥ ♥ ♥

11 When you walk into a party with him, do you cringe if there are other hot chicks there?

__**a.** No!

__**b.** And leave—usually alone.

__**c.** Only when he hits on them in front of you.

12 Does he greet a surprising number of girls by name?

__**a.** Yes.

__**b.** Sometimes.

__**c.** No.

♥ ♥ ♥

13 Does he say, "Hi, beautiful," to strangers?

__**a.** No.

__**b.** Yes.

__**c.** He thinks it's friendly.

ANSWERS

MAJOR DROOLER

1. A	6. C	11. B
2. C	7. C	12. A
3. A	8. A	13. B
4. C	9. A	
5. C	10. C	

QUESTIONABLE BEHAVIOR

1. B	6. B	11. C
2. B	7. A	12. B
3. C	8. A	13. C
4. B	9. B	
5. B	10. B	

"GUY STUFF"

1. C	6. A	11. A
2. A	7. B	12. C
3. B	8. B	13. A
4. A	9. C	
5. A	10. A	

should you give him a
SECOND CHANCE?

Okay, so he made out with your best friend behind the field house. Is that reason enough to end it forever? Or should you forgive him? Below is a list of fictional situations in which formerly lovable guys screw up! Check your willingness to forgive—or to totally forget about it.

■■■■■■■■■■■■■■■■■■■■■■■■■■■■■■

1 **He dumped you the night before**

__**a.** your prom.

__**b.** your sister's wedding.

__**c.** the school dance.

2 **You opened his locker and found**

__**a.** your photo removed.

__**b.** a love poem from someone else.

__**c.** a new girl's telephone number.

3 **Lately when you're in a clinch, his attention seems to wander. Last night he**

__**a.** called you by someone else's name when locking lips.

__**b.** said he was coming down with a cold and ducked out.

__**c.** asked if you had any Tic Tacs.

♥ ♥ ♥

4 **You reached under his pillow and found**

__**a.** his yearbook.

__**b.** *Playboy.*

__**c.** a photo of his old girlfriend.

♥ ♥ ♥

5 **He says he can't see you this weekend because he's going on a retreat. Later you**

__**a.** discover him with his arm around a pretty girl at the multiplex.

__**b.** hear he hooked up with someone else.

__**c.** learn he's very spiritual.

6 **He borrows twenty dollars from you, then**

__**a.** treats his buds to pizza.

__**b.** goes to a basketball game.

__**c.** takes a date to the movies.

♥ ♥ ♥

7 **You open a jewelry box sitting on his dresser. In it, there's**

__**a.** a gold engraved locket with someone else's initials.

__**b.** a piece of cotton.

__**c.** a birthstone bracelet that's not for your month.

♥ ♥ ♥

8 **His diary is conveniently left around. When he goes to make nachos, you read it and discover**

__**a.** he's a terrific writer.

__**b.** his life is boring.

__**c.** he has a passionate crush on your sister.

9 You walk into his house with him, and his mother shouts from another room, "Brooke called three times and says Friday is okay." You

__**a.** watch him turn red.

__**b.** remember he said Brooke was his old baby-sitter.

__**c.** realize that's why he didn't ask you out for that night.

♥ ♥ ♥

10 Your girlfriends report that your guy had asked the most popular girl in your class to the winter formal, but she turned him down. So he asked you. Do you

__**a.** go anyway—you have a new dress?

__**b.** call it off?

__**c.** get bummed out at your friends?

SCORING

1. If you answered A or B, both are trouble. You've gone to expense—especially for the prom—that's unforgivable.

2. All are bad but not grounds for total dismissal.

3. B might be real, but A is unforgivable. C says something about you.

4. A and B are normal. C is mighty suspicious, but he could weasel out of it.

5. B is totally unforgivable.

6. C is the breakup bummer.

7. A and C demand pretty convincing explanations.

8. C—he obviously wants you to know but doesn't want to do it face-to-face.

9. A and C are pretty incriminating—time for a serious break.

10. B and C.

TOP HONORS:
what does your
dream boy do for you?

Besides playing with the family pet or fixing Mom's computer, what are some other ways guys make you feel good? There are at least two dozen sweet things buried in the list below. Can you spot them?

■ ■

Check the good things:

❑ **1** Saying your hair looks good

❑ **2** Coming over when you're sick

❑ **3** Borrowing your homework

❑ **4** Leaving surprises in your locker

❑ **5** Misplacing your cell phone

❑ **6** Giving you his jacket when you're cold

❑ **7** Leaving parties when you want

❑ **8** Messing up your room

❑ **9** Eating all your favorite snacks

❑ **10** Emptying the fridge

❑ **11** Renting your favorite tapes

❑ **12** Giving you back rubs

❑ **13** Asking about your girlfriends

❑ **14** Avoiding your girlfriends

❑ **15** Surprising you with tiny gifts

❑ **16** Keeping you up late talking about nothing

❑ **17** Returning your class notes messed up

❑ **18** Cleaning your dad's car

❑ **19** Knowing your favorite albums

❑ **20** Visiting your relatives with you

❑ **21** Pigging out on your dime

❑ **22** Taking you sledding

❑ **23** Calling you up after your favorite TV shows

❑ **24** Hanging around when you're tired

❑ **25** Helping you with your volunteer work

❑ **26** Reading your essays

❑ **27** Having burping contests with your brother

❏ **28** Setting up your new CD player

❏ **29** Loving your cooking

❏ **30** Making long-term plans

❏ **31** Showing up late

❏ **32** Acting wild with his buds

❏ **33** Encouraging you

❏ **34** Bringing you treats

❏ **35** Playing the games you like

❏ **36** Giving you a sweet, special nickname

ANSWERS

Two Dozen Great Things

1. #1	9. #15	17. #27
2. #2	10. #18	18. #28
3. #4	11. #19	19. #29
4. #6	12. #20	20. #30
5. #7	13. #22	21. #33
6. #11	14. #23	22. #34
7. #12	15. #25	23. #35
8. #13	16. #26	24. #36

CRUSH-NAPPING:
are you **TEMPTED** to
steal your **bud's guy**?

Yes, putting the make on your bud's guy may be as bad for you as a week's worth of detention, but there's something about this boy that's got you going weak in the knees. Is he sending signals? Could it all be in your head? And—very important—could your bud and her guy be really solid? Find out if you can read between the lines by checking off the answer that best fits the situation.

- -

1 **He talks to me all the time.**

❏ Looks Good for You
❏ Looks Good for Her

2 **My bud complains about him.**

❏ Looks Good for You
❏ Looks Good for Her

3 He made a U-turn when he saw me walking my dog.
❏ Looks Good for You
❏ Looks Good for Her

4 He gave her a heart necklace last week.
❏ Looks Good for You
❏ Looks Good for Her

5 He always sits next to her at lunch.
❏ Looks Good for You
❏ Looks Good for Her

6 My laptop was jammed and he fixed it.
❏ Looks Good for You
❏ Looks Good for Her

7 He told his bud to say hi for him to me.
❏ Looks Good for You
❏ Looks Good for Her

8 His parents invited her to dinner.
❏ Looks Good for You
❏ Looks Good for Her

9 I went to the movies with them and he sat in the middle.
❏ Looks Good for You
❏ Looks Good for Her

10 Last week, he watched my soccer game.
❏ Looks Good for You
❏ Looks Good for Her

11 I caught him staring at her in bio.
❏ Looks Good for You
❏ Looks Good for Her

12 My bud gave him a birthday party.
❏ Looks Good for You
❏ Looks Good for Her

13 When I ran into him in the video store, he waited until I got my tape, then walked me home.
❑ Looks Good for You
❑ Looks Good for Her

14 When we were taking yearbook photos, he always put his arm around her.
❑ Looks Good for You
❑ Looks Good for Her

15 He hung up new photos of her in his locker.
❑ Looks Good for You
❑ Looks Good for Her

16 He wrote her a poem.
❑ Looks Good for You
❑ Looks Good for Her

17 She's going to Spain for the summer and isn't upset about not seeing him.
❑ Looks Good for You
❑ Looks Good for Her

18 At the Latin Club fund-raiser car wash, he kept dousing me with water.
❑ Looks Good for You
❑ Looks Good for Her

19 He cleans his car before going to see her.
❑ Looks Good for You
❑ Looks Good for Her

20 They always dance to "their" song.
❑ Looks Good for You
❑ Looks Good for Her

SCORING

Mostly "LOOKS GOOD FOR YOU"

Hm-mmm. Well, girl, it could be time to release the inner vixen. Their duo may be getting a little flat, but it's never wise to be too aggressive. Take a wait-and-see attitude, 'cause if he likes you more and more, he'll start sending you stronger and stronger signals. Be careful of your bud's feelings—she's important and you don't want to mess up a good friendship.

Mostly "LOOKS GOOD FOR HER"

Slam on the brakes now and pull that love boat into dry dock! Especially if he recently did something major like gave her jewelry, wrote a poem, or invited her to meet his parents, he could just be so gone on her, he wants to be friends with her friends. Or he could just be a big slobbery type, like a golden retriever who loves everyone.

chapter THREE
DATING

Blind dates, first dates, prom dates, love on the rebound dates, double dates—it seems there are more kinds of dates than Tori Spelling has hairstyles. Here's where we'll check out many dating scenarios to make sure you're prepared for taking your crush public.

GROWTH CHART:
are you getting
better at dating?

Let's see how far you've come since you first got thoughts of bagging a guy. The situations below typically arise on the dating scene. How do you rate how well they're played? Use 1 (rookie) through 5 (expert). Let's go!

1	2	3	4	5

1 The new hottie you've been cruising says he "might" drop by that evening. You tell him not to be disappointed if you've already gone out.

2 It's your third date, so you decide it's okay to dress down in your scruffiest jeans.

	1	2	3	4	5

3 You're going out to an expensive restaurant, so you pig out and order a lot of different dishes. After all, he must be able to afford it.

4 You forget that he likes long hair and show up with yours in a tight bun.

5 You forget that you're meeting his parents and show up in an ultrasexy outfit.

6 You run into his buddies on your first date. You laugh and act like it's perfectly fine.

7 When he says he doesn't know where you're going on your date, you tell him to call you a couple of days in advance.

1	2	3	4	5

8 At the big dance, you spend lots of time talking to your girlfriends.

9 Even though he's asked you out, you still don't believe he likes you, so you put a chock-block on being natural.

10 You're running late and haven't had time to shower and dress. You ask him to wait.

11 He drops by for an impromptu picnic—with food and all. You go for it.

12 When he takes you to a drinking party, you ask to leave after twenty minutes.

ANSWERS

1. Expert #5: Those who know how to play the game don't let others set their schedules for them.

2. Rookie #1 to 2: Beginners err in taking things for granted.

3. Rookie #1 to 2: Only rookies overindulge in front of a new beau.

4. Rookie #1: Beginners often make basic mistakes like forgetting how to please.

5. Rookie #1: Real pros don't embarrass his parents.

6. Expert #5: Experts never display annoyance over losing an exclusive.

7. Midrange #3 to 5: On-the-job training—you want to know how to plan.

8. Midrange #2 to 4: Trainees often retreat to school-yard habits.

9. Midrange #2 to 4: Trainees can still be insecure.

10. Expert #5: You always want to look your best.

11. Expert #5: When he puts himself out, experts know it.

12. Expert #5: You know how to avoid conflict.

Should you be **FRIENDS with BENEFITS?**

Friend with a bonus? Fun on the side? Here are ten questions to ask yourself to find out whether this risky scenario is really the best way to find happiness.

1 Was this "booty call without commitment" your idea or his?

_____

_____

_____

2 If it was his, what was his reasoning?

_____

_____

_____

3 How do you justify it?

_____

_____

_____

4 After a hookup, do you feel used, unhappy—or satisfied?

_____
_____
_____

5 Do you ever ditch the girls for a quick hookup?

_____
_____
_____

6 Does he treat you well in public?

_____
_____
_____

7 Have you told your friends about it? Do his friends know? Why is it a secret?

_____
_____
_____

8 How long has this been going on? A week, month, or year?

_____

_____

9 Were you friends before the benefit sessions started?

_____

_____

_____

10 If you end the bonus, will you still be friends?

_____

_____

_____

ANSWERS

1. Make sure you realize whether this situation was your idea or his. If it was yours, that is different from going by his rules. Make sure you want to be in this scenario.

2. What was his reasoning? Let's get this right—he doesn't want to commit, but stay friends, but still hook up? Could it be because he just broke up? Or is he too busy with school and extracurricular activities? Maybe he wants to get to know you better first. His reasoning is a great indication of how he feels. Perhaps he is enjoying the booty but doesn't want to be serious. What does that say about his feelings for you as a person?

3. Do you justify the situation by wanting to keep your options open until someone else comes along? Maybe you like him, and you're hoping he'll start to want you more as a girlfriend. If you are doing it to make someone else jealous, that is without a doubt the wrong reason. Consider your motives and what you are getting out of this "relationship."

4. If you're unhappy after a hookup, then it needs to stop. There is no reason for feeling bad about yourself. If he makes you feel like anything less than a goddess, this is a "no go."

5. If you are ditching the girls for a quick hookup, reevaluate your priorities. Your girlfriends offer you something of real value—support and loyalty.

6. The way he treats you in public is revealing. Even more so if you are keeping it secretive. If you're not his "girlfriend," most likely he won't treat you like one.

7. If you haven't told your friends or he hasn't told his, think about why he's keeping it on the low. If you really do care about each other, it shouldn't have to be a covert operation. If he really cares about you, shouldn't he be proud of you and want to show you off?

8. If this has been going on for only a week, there might be potential for him to realize he wants more than booty. But if he's set in his benefit mode, abort the mission entirely. A long-term "friends with benefits" can be emotionally debilitating and may compromise your character and sense of self-worth.

9. If you weren't friends before, than most likely he hasn't gotten the chance to get to know you for you. Offer to spend some time without the play to make sure his ulterior motives aren't overshadowing his getting to know a great person.

10. If you yelled, "Pull over!" and broke off the booty, and he stuck around, then of course you would know he likes you. But if he hit the road, then you would realize the opposite was true. Consider this, if he really likes you and wants to be with you, then why aren't you together as a couple?

can you **HANDLE** the prom?

More than likely, even supertogether chicks like Meadow Soprano and Kelly Taylor would have some flutters when it comes to the big occasions, like *the prom*. This is the Super Bowl of high school social events and whether you're going with your steady, a new crush, your cousin twice removed, or a blind date, you need to be prepared. To put your best foot forward on the big night, take our quiz below by matching up column A to the right answer in column B.

■■■■■■■■■■■■■■■■■■■■■■■■■■■■■■■■

Column A

___**1.** Your first prom

___**2.** A chain-link dress

___**3.** Superearly curfew

___**4.** Sharing a limo

Column B

a. It's a necessity.

b. Your date is Marilyn Manson.

c. Parental POV

d. Best way to have fun

Column A

_____ **5.** No drinking/ no smoking

_____ **6.** At least five trips to the mall

_____ **7.** Backup pair of sandals

_____ **8.** Flower consultation

_____ **9.** "It's too expensive!"

_____ **10.** "What a nut!"

_____ **11.** President of the Honor Society

_____ **12.** Steve Tyler

_____ **13.** Jennifer Love Hewitt

_____ **14.** Jennifer Lopez

Column B

e. Standard operating procedure

f. Matching posies

g. Parents taking photos

h. Lots of dancing

i. Your parents hate your date.

j. Safest way to go

k. Date's fiscal responsibility

l. Tight, low-cut gown

m. Grandma's dream date

n. Mom's dream date for daughter

o. Dad won't let you out of the house.

p. They're losers.

Column A

___ **15.** Prom king and
queen

___ **16.** You're prom
queen.

___ **17.** Lots of new
makeup

___ **18.** New appreciation
of the Oscar
ceremony

___ **19.** Breakfast at
four A.M.

___ **20.** Sleep

Column B

q. "Wow!"

r. A great way to preview
fashion

s. Postprom party
hopping

t. For the rest of the
weekend

ANSWERS

1. G	6. E	11. N	16. Q
2. B	7. H	12. M	17. A
3. I	8. F	13. L	18. R
4. J	9. C	14. O	19. S
5. D	10. K	15. P	20. T

is it **SAFE** to fall for a **GUY** who's on the **REBOUND?**

What's sadder—a hottie with a broken heart or a sick puppy? If you said the hottie, then you're probably right. The recently singled have special needs, but sometimes rushing in with first-aid love medicine can backfire and you can get hurt next. So if you want to avoid being a victim of your own impulses, diagnose how well you can read love's vital signs. Check "Green Light" if you think the situation should be allowed to go on, "Red" if it should stop.

■■■■■■■■■■■■■■■■■■■■■■■■■■■■■■■■

	GREEN LIGHT	RED LIGHT
1 It's your first date and he doesn't want to take it slow.	____	____
2 His ex's name pops up a lot—from him!	____	____
3 You heard through the grapevine that he's still crushing on her.	____	____

	GREEN LIGHT	RED LIGHT
4 In study hall, you catch him doodling her name.	_____	_____
5 He wants to introduce you as his "girlfriend" right away.	_____	_____
6 He phones three or four times a night.	_____	_____
7 "Girls are trouble" is his new motto.	_____	_____
8 In terms of love talk, he's using the *L* word pretty fast.	_____	_____
9 You bumped into his old obsession in gym. She says she's so relieved it's over.	_____	_____
10 You hear he bounces from one crush to the next.	_____	_____
11 His favorite role models are Bill Clinton, Donald Trump, and Hugh Hefner.	_____	_____
12 His mother calls you "Dear"—she can't remember all his girls' names!	_____	_____

ANSWERS

ALL THE ANSWERS SHOULD BE "RED LIGHT"!

Don't you be the one to run a red light—beware of guys who can't spend ten minutes alone. He's trying to transfer everything onto a new chick right away, and he's missing the point. You're someone unique—not just his love ointment to soothe his wounds. Be wary especially if he introduces you as his "girlfriend" right away.

If you answered "GREEN LIGHT"—you obviously like him lots—maybe you waited for the breakup. And you're willing to overlook what others may consider danger signs to have him. Make sure your relationship progresses into something that relates solely to you—not to his girls in the past.

what guy QUALITIES do it for you?

Besides his being in the top 10 percent of the class and having the cutest butt you've ever watched bounce across the gym floor, what other meaningful qualities do you seek in a guy? If you've never asked yourself this tantalizing question, please be our guest with this "great guy qualities" quiz. Below are lots of neat things about the opposite sex—rate the qualities that are important to you on a scale of 1 to 10, with 1 being the least important and 10 the most.

____ **a.** Buff body

____ **b.** Great hair

____ **c.** Speaks a foreign language

____ **d.** Loves dogs

____ **e.** Has his own car

____ **f.** Thinks you're funny

____ **g.** Adores the way you smell

____ **h.** Writes you romantic letters

____ **i.** Hates body piercing and tattoos

____ **j.** Calls your mother "Mom"

____ **k.** Sends you mushy cards

____ **l.** Comes back after fights

____ **m.** Wears old clothes

____ **n.** Follows the latest fashion

____ **o.** Saves his money for school

____ **p.** Gets you great gifts

____ **q.** Loves to hear you sing

____ **r.** Says your smile makes you even prettier

____ **s.** Can fix things

____ **t.** Loves to shop

____ **u.** Has sexy eyes

____ **v.** Calls after you get together

____ **w.** Goes to his kid sister's plays

____ **x.** Makes the honor roll

____ **y.** Visits old teachers

____ **z.** Can say "I love you" in Latin

SCORING

Did you rate A, B, E, N, P, T, and U the most important? These are all about appearances. It would seem as though you're into looks—and you want a guy you're proud to be seen with.

If you rated C, H, I, L, O, W, X, and Z the most important, you like more intellectual guys who are into achievement and plan for the future. You go for guys who are careful and considerate.

If you rated D, F, G, J, K, M, Q, R, S, V, and Y the most important, you've picked Mr. Sensitive. He's about as comfortable and friendly as an old pair of jeans—and will more than likely never break your heart.

If you rated all the qualities high, then you really love guys! Have fun finding Mr. Right!

what is a
GREAT FIRST DATE?

Hola! You and your crush are going out! Whether it's because you made the move on him or vice versa, first dates are always important. You want to have fun for sure, but you also want to know how to make yourself the main attraction. More than likely, you'll have lots of "first dates" in your life, so read on to see what makes a first date successful.

Rate the dates by checking one choice:

1 Bowling
- ❏ Great!
- ❏ So-So
- ❏ Could Tank
- ❏ Not on a Bet!

2 Driving range for golf
- ❏ Great!
- ❏ So-So
- ❏ Could Tank
- ❏ Not on a Bet!

3 Lunch with his mom
❑ Great!
❑ So-So
❑ Could Tank
❑ Not on a Bet!

4 Visit to an aquarium
❑ Great!
❑ So-So
❑ Could Tank
❑ Not on a Bet!

5 Barbecue
❑ Great!
❑ So-So
❑ Could Tank
❑ Not on a Bet!

6 Movies
❑ Great!
❑ So-So
❑ Could Tank
❑ Not on a Bet!

7 Sporting event
❑ Great!
❑ So-So
❑ Could Tank
❑ Not on a Bet!

8 Wedding
❑ Great!
❑ So-So
❑ Could Tank
❑ Not on a Bet!

9 The prom
❑ Great!
❑ So-So
❑ Could Tank
❑ Not on a Bet!

10 The mall
❑ Great!
❑ So-So
❑ Could Tank
❑ Not on a Bet!

11 Parade
❑ Great!
❑ So-So
❑ Could Tank
❑ Not on a Bet!

12 School play
❑ Great!
❑ So-So
❑ Could Tank
❑ Not on a Bet!

13 Your ex-boyfriend's birthday party
❑ Great!
❑ So-So
❑ Could Tank
❑ Not on a Bet!

14 Pool party
❑ Great!
❑ So-So
❑ Could Tank
❑ Not on a Bet!

15 Dance club
❑ Great!
❑ So-So
❑ Could Tank
❑ Not on a Bet!

16 Visit to a science fair
❑ Great!
❑ So-So
❑ Could Tank
❑ Not on a Bet!

17 Sleep-over party
❑ Great!
❑ So-So
❑ Could Tank
❑ Not on a Bet!

18 Volleyball at the beach
❑ Great!
❑ So-So
❑ Could Tank
❑ Not on a Bet!

19 Sailing
❑ Great!
❑ So-So
❑ Could Tank
❑ Not on a Bet!

20 Walk in a beautiful garden
❑ Great!
❑ So-So
❑ Could Tank
❑ Not on a Bet!

21 Shopping at a discount warehouse
❑ Great!
❑ So-So
❑ Could Tank
❑ Not on a Bet!

22 Pottery workshop
❑ Great!
❑ So-So
❑ Could Tank
❑ Not on a Bet!

23 Whale watch
❑ Great!
❑ So-So
❑ Could Tank
❑ Not on a Bet!

24 Visit to a historic home site
❑ Great!
❑ So-So
❑ Could Tank
❑ Not on a Bet!

25 Hanging in his bud's basement
❑ Great!
❑ So-So
❑ Could Tank
❑ Not on a Bet!

ANSWERS

GREAT!
1, 2, 4, 5, 7, 11, 20, 22, 23, 24

SO-SO
6, 10, 12, 14, 16, 21

COULD TANK
9, 13, 15, 18, 19, 25

NOT ON A BET!
3, 8, 17

If you got "Great!" mostly right, scopes up for you socially. You know how to see what's on the date horizon. The key to a great time is keeping him aware of you while you get to know him better. Always try to stay away from too many diversions--a pool party, for instance, gives him the opportunity to check out other chicks, as does a dance club and volleyball on the beach. Also, going out with his mom is *not* a date! Places where you can't really talk won't help you, like the movies or the school play. If you really like your date, something that promises hands-on fun is interesting, like a pottery lesson (think *Ghost*) or shooting golf balls together. Doing something that involves nature, like visiting a garden, a whale watch, or a visit to an aquarium, lets you see if he has a sensitive side. A parade is both exciting and low maintenance. First date for a prom is risky—it's too filled with tension—and an ex's birthday could be uptight and could easily tank.

can you spot a
date bummer
before it happens?

While we sincerely hope that every date you go on is superfun and special, we must be realistic. There may be times you wish you had had a warning. Most guys mean well, but sometimes, they propose things that are so destined to bomb, you can smell disaster three weeks away. To avoid such date pitfalls, take the quiz below. Match up each sceriano with the behavior that best describes a, b, and c.

■ ■

1 He wants to go to the hottest new movie in town and insists the nine P.M. show won't be crowded. You

	POOR SPORT	GOOD SPOTTING	FINE FORM
a. say you have to arrive early.	_____	_____	_____
b. tell him he's wrong but go anyway.	_____	_____	_____
c. mope when you can't get in.	_____	_____	_____

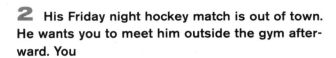

2 His Friday night hockey match is out of town. He wants you to meet him outside the gym afterward. You

	POOR SPORT	GOOD SPOTTING	FINE FORM
a. leave in a huff if he's ten minutes late.	____	____	____
b. ask to meet at the library so you can wait inside if he's late.	____	____	____
c. give him your cell phone number to call you when he's ready.	____	____	____

3 While his parents are out of town, he suggests going to his place. You

	POOR SPORT	GOOD SPOTTING	FINE FORM
a. agree, but tell him you want company.	____	____	____
b. say you'll take a rain check.	____	____	____
c. go but stay on the phone with your friends the whole time.	____	____	____

4 It's your first Saturday night back from camp and you can't wait to see him. When he shows up forty-five minutes late, you

	POOR SPORT	GOOD SPOTTING	FINE FORM
a. jump on his back instantly for not being "serious."	___	___	___
b. ask him what delayed him.	___	___	___
c. show him the photos of the cute guys you met.	___	___	___

5 You hate sushi. He knows it. Your double date is meeting you—guess where? Yoshi's Sushi Buffet. What do you do?

	POOR SPORT	GOOD SPOTTING	FINE FORM
a. Tell everyone about the latest raw fish scare.	___	___	___
b. Order rice.	___	___	___
c. Make him stop on the way for a slice of pizza.	___	___	___

6 You arrive at his house for a barbecue only to discover his dad has opened the pool. You hold back because your thighs are as hairy as a dozen kiwis. You

	POOR SPORT	GOOD SPOTTING	FINE FORM
a. call a taxi.	___	___	___
b. offer to make tacos.	___	___	___
c. say you have an ear infection and ask him to take you to the drugstore– in the mall, where you can enjoy an afternoon of shopping instead.	___	___	___

7 Lately, he's been asking lots of questions about your best friend, Mia. When he suggests double-dating, you

	POOR SPORT	GOOD SPOTTING	FINE FORM
a. explain it's time to see other people.	___	___	___
b. blow up and accuse him of wandering, then make him miserable all day.	___	___	___
c. tell him she's volunteering at a local shelter and ask him to take some leftovers down there.	___	___	___

8 He has an impromptu urge to take you someplace special, so he gives you the names of restaurants and asks you to call for a reservation. You

	POOR SPORT	GOOD SPOTTING	FINE FORM
a. remind him gently that this is his treat.	⎯⎯	⎯⎯	⎯⎯
b. reserve a table for eleven P.M. and then yawn through dinner.	⎯⎯	⎯⎯	⎯⎯
c. ask him to make you brunch instead.	⎯⎯	⎯⎯	⎯⎯

ANSWERS

1. a. Good spotting
   b. Fine form
   c. Poor sport

2. a. Poor sport
   b. Good spotting
   c. Fine form

3. a. Good spotting
   b. Fine form
   c. Poor sport

4. a. Poor sport
   b. Good spotting
   c. Fine form

5. a. Fine form
   b. Good spotting
   c. Poor sport

6. a. Poor sport
   b. Good spotting
   c. Fine form

7. a. Fine form
   b. Poor sport
   c. Good spotting

8. a. Good spotting
   b. Poor sport
   c. Fine form

If you're in fine form, you don't let others bend you out of shape. You always rise above disappointments, so it doesn't become a messy blow. You're not afraid to stand up for yourself.

If you're good at spotting, you see the potential for disaster and in a good-humored way try to avert it.

Poor you, poor sport. You've got a lot to learn, but dating is practice. Don't let others' behavior rattle you so much. You'll feel better if you can laugh at things—and him.

BLIND DATE:
Serious Handicap
or **Guiding Light?**

Quick—next to public speaking—what's the thing you most dread? If you replied, "Blind dates," then you're like the rest of us. Many times they're DOA, but they don't have to be. Sometimes they can pan out into something more enjoyable. See if you can spot the ways to make them better. Check one answer.

■■■■■■■■■■■■■■■■■■■■■■■■■■■■■■■■

1 **Your girlfriend always raves about her out-of-town cousin. Now she's egging you to go with him to the prom. You**

__**a.** turn up the volume on the CD player.

__**b.** tell her you'll be studying that night.

__**c.** ask to talk to him on the phone first.

2 Your dad's old college roommate has a son who wants to take you out. You

___**a.** check out his yearbook photos.

___**b.** ask your dad's advice.

___**c.** blow him off.

♥ ♥ ♥

3 You go on a blind date and really dig the guy! Do you

___**a.** act like blind dates are a drag?

___**b.** tell him you're pleasantly surprised?

___**c.** ask for his phone number?

♥ ♥ ♥

4 You're on a blind date and you run into your former honey. You

___**a.** act like you're with a stranger.

___**b.** introduce them.

___**c.** head for the nearest ladies' room.

5 You arrange to meet your date at the movies. When you arrive, you notice the only guy there is playing with a Nintendo and looks so geeky. You

___**a.** dive behind the popcorn machine.

___**b.** give him a chance and say hi.

___**c.** tell him you have a very contagious skin disease.

6 The date's been going so great. Now it's time to say good-bye. You

___**a.** ask for his cell phone number and e-mail address.

___**b.** pull out your calendar.

___**c.** say you'd love to hear from him.

7 Well, the date could have been fun. But his biting sense of humor annoyed you at times. Do you

___**a.** stare at his lower lip, then say there are inexpensive cures for cold sores?

___**b.** tell him you're volunteering for a "Teens in Space" program and have to get home early?

___**c.** say good-bye and leave him intact?

8 You passed up a blind date with him because you heard he was a nerd, but when you met him weeks later at a party, you flipped! How do you get him to go out on a date now?

__**a.** You tell him you've fully recovered from your bout of bronchitis.

__**b.** Mention that you're headed to Victoria's Secret and could use some advice.

__**c.** Make him laugh and enjoy your company.

9 You go to your aunt's wedding with a blind date, but he meets someone else there and dances nonstop with her. You

__**a.** eat his slice of wedding cake.

__**b.** leave without saying good-bye.

__**c.** find another way home.

10 Your blind date takes you to a superhot make-out movie. You

__**a.** spend the night pulling him off you.

__**b.** spill soda on the floor.

__**c.** move way down front.

ANSWERS

1. C: Chatting with a prospective date on the phone gives you a little more info.

2. A or B: Homework first could save trouble later.

3. B: Being light and positive helps ensure repeat dates.

4. B: Introduce them. Your old flame won't care and having a former beau around could add to your allure.

5. B: He deserves a chance, that's part of going on a "blind" date.

6. C: Let him know you like him but don't act desperate.

7. C: Even if your date mistakenly thinks he's superwitty, just let it go.

8. C: Show him what he missed.

9. C: Sometimes leaving gracefully is the best thing you can do.

10. C: This should put you on display and hamper any thoughts of making out.

FLIRTING 101:
are you **Miss Leading Joker** or the **Queen of Hearts?**

Do you lead guys on or are you a straight shooter? Take this quiz to find out if you have what it takes to be a flirting champion.

■■■■■■■■■■■■■■■■■■■■■■■■■■■■■

Answer yes or no to the following questions and then check out the answers below for more info.

	YES	NO
1 When you meet a potential crush, do you ask his name straight off?	___	___
2 If you see him across the room and feel a good vibe, are you likely to introduce yourself?	___	___
3 Would you ever give a new guy your digits right away?	___	___
4 Would you ask for his?	___	___

	YES	NO
5 Would you ever flirt with his friends to make him jealous?	___	___
6 Do you ask your friends for background info on him?	___	___
7 Is brushing against him on the dance floor the way to his heart?	___	___
8 Do you find ways to figure out his favorite food/candy and then surprise him with it in class?	___	___
9 Would you ever offer to give him a lift?	___	___
10 Do you ask him questions about himself?	___	___
11 Do you prefer to dominate the conversation?	___	___
12 Do you send yourself chocolates or flowers to make him jealous?	___	___

YES   NO

13 Do you consider playing hard to get an effective flirting strategy?   _____   _____

14 Would you ever break plans with him at the last minute to make him think you're too busy?   _____   _____

15 If your friend got his number for you, would you ever call him the next day?   _____   _____

ANSWERS

1. Asking his name straight out exudes confidence, which is always a turn-on as well as a great flirting strategy. In doing so, you can address him more personally with "It was wonderful to meet you, Dan," instead of, "Nice to meet you." That extra personal bit will make you stick in his mind.

2. If you are sensing a positive vibe, go ahead and introduce yourself. You can't gain any yardage if you don't advance past the line of scrimmage.

3. Handing him your digits can both be misleading and lead to his heart. The way in which you approach the situation is important. Steer clear of writing them on his body. Instead, simply write them on a napkin or sheet of paper. Now the ball is in his court.

4. Asking for his number is a great move. Be careful, however, of giving out your e-mail address until you know him better.

5. Flirting with his friends to make him jealous is a bad move. Play it straight and focus on the one you are interested in. He may get confused and ultimately turned off.

6. Asking a friend for info on him is a good way to gain perspective. Just make sure to keep his or her words separate from your own opinion. To be a real sweetheart, listen to others, but make your own judgments.

7. Brushing against him on the dance floor can send him some positive signals that you are digging him, but make sure not to be overly aggressive. Groping him could make him think you are interested in a simply physical relationship.

8. Showing up in class with his favorite candy or snack will start a conversation and open the opportunity to share a bag of chips with him. This is a great way to interact and a safe move.

9. Go ahead, offer him a ride home, but only if you're with others. He will recognize your generosity, and this move shows you are willing to go out of your way to help him out. Also, you can find out where he lives for scoping later.

10. Make sure you ask about him. Instead of saying, "How are you?" ask, "What did you do over the summer?" From that direction, he can't cop-out with "I'm fine." He'll have to have a quasi-conversation with you regardless.

11. Make sure not to dominate the conversation. No one wants to be trapped in a one-sided conversation. If you continue to gab, he might tune you out.

12. While you might think sending yourself gifts may lure him in, he may see you are "taken" and hit the road.

13. Playing hard to get might be effective sometimes, but most of the time, playing it straight and being yourself will benefit you in the long run.

14. Breaking plans with anyone at the last minute is a bad move. Especially when trying to flirt and make a good impression on a guy. Being inconsiderate will only chase him away.

15. If you get his number from a friend, feel free to call. But be prepared for him to ask how you got his number. To ease the situation, have a Plan B in place in case he flops—like you called up just to ask him a chemistry question.

how do you
ASK A GUY OUT?

If there's a new love who's been using a lot of your memory space lately, but getting him to ask you out is as hard as acing calculus, why not ask him out instead? Take our test below to see if you're up to it.

■ ■

1 What's the most mature approach to asking a guy out?

___**a.** E-mail.

___**b.** Telephone.

___**c.** Face-to-face.

2 What if you broadcast the idea first with your buds?

___**a.** That's okay—you're going to tell them anyway.

___**b.** Bad idea—it could get back to him.

___**c.** Maybe if he finds out, he'll ask you out first.

3 You rehearse what you're going to say to him how many times?

__**a.** None. You want to appear natural.

__**b.** You'll write it down.

__**c.** At least a dozen.

4 You invite your crush out, and he replies, "I'll think about it, can I get back to you?" Your response is

__**a.** a deep red blush.

__**b.** a thought crime.

__**c.** a smooth, "Let me know in two days or I'll have to make other plans."

5 It's prom time and your heartthrob is— guess what?—a younger man! Is it okay to ask him out?

__**a.** Only if he is very mature for his age.

__**b.** No, you'll look lame.

__**c.** Yes, it's flattering and he'll probably want to go.

6 In class, you're planning to pass a note to your fantasy boy asking him to the fall formal. What if the teacher busts you?

__**a.** You would remind him of everyone's right to privacy.

__**b.** Ouch!

__**c.** Your crush would know you really like him.

7 You're crushing on him so big time—what's a special way to let him know you want to go out?

__**a.** Put a sweet note in his locker.

__**b.** Leave lots of messages on his answering machine.

__**c.** Tell his friends how great you are.

8 You like this guy, but you're spinning your wheels. Is he shy or does he really not care? You

__**a.** find a pressure-free way to be alone with him—like suddenly appearing by the gym after practice.

__**b.** ask if he's seen the newest teen flick.

__**c.** follow him on the lunch line every day for a week.

9 You're really working it—taking an interest in his activities, like attending rehearsals for the upcoming school concert where he has a violin solo. Could this lead to a date payoff?

__**a.** Yes, it gives you things in common.

__**b.** No, it's too obvious.

__**c.** Only if he wakes up.

10 You don't drive. What's the best kind of date to ask him on—where you can avoid end-of-the-evening discomfort?

__**a.** Have Mom drive you to and from the date.

__**b.** Hire a car service.

__**c.** Go out with a group of friends so you can drive home together.

ANSWERS

1. C: A face-to-face invitation may be tough, but it's the best way to see his reaction—it could be a wonderful smile.

2. A: You know you're going to tell your friends, so don't beat yourself up for it.

3. More than likely it will be C.

4. C: Remember, you took the risk, but don't let him control you.

5. C: Why not? He's probably only a year or two younger, and has lots to offer—otherwise you wouldn't be interested, right?

6. A: Only do this if you really can handle getting busted.

7. B: is annoying, C is transparent, but A could do it.

8. A: If that doesn't work, think about moving on.

9. A: The more connections you have, the better.

10. C: This takes the parents out of the picture.

Rate the Dates:
sizzle or fizzle?

You sign on and—guess what?—"You've got mail." It's your guy wanting to get together, and he promises you'll have fun! Can you predict what will rock or what will flop? Below is a list of potential date opportunities. Rate them 1 (The Worst!), 2 (Okay), or 3 (The Best).

1 Make-out movie
- ❑ 1 (The Worst!)
- ❑ 2 (Okay)
- ❑ 3 (The Best)

2 Balloon ride
- ❑ 1 (The Worst!)
- ❑ 2 (Okay)
- ❑ 3 (The Best)

3 Water adventure park
- ❑ 1 (The Worst!)
- ❑ 2 (Okay)
- ❑ 3 (The Best)

4 Four-wheeling with buds
- ❑ 1 (The Worst!)
- ❑ 2 (Okay)
- ❑ 3 (The Best)

5 Horseback riding
❑ 1 (The Worst!)
❑ 2 (Okay)
❑ 3 (The Best)

6 Pigging out at an ice cream parlor
❑ 1 (The Worst!)
❑ 2 (Okay)
❑ 3 (The Best)

7 Rollerblading
❑ 1 (The Worst!)
❑ 2 (Okay)
❑ 3 (The Best)

8 Taking his car to inspection
❑ 1 (The Worst!)
❑ 2 (Okay)
❑ 3 (The Best)

9 Backpacking
❑ 1 (The Worst!)
❑ 2 (Okay)
❑ 3 (The Best)

10 Dinner with his grandparents
❑ 1 (The Worst!)
❑ 2 (Okay)
❑ 3 (The Best)

11 Pizza parlor with his buds
❑ 1 (The Worst!)
❑ 2 (Okay)
❑ 3 (The Best)

12 Window shopping at the mall
❑ 1 (The Worst!)
❑ 2 (Okay)
❑ 3 (The Best)

13 Karaoke session
❑ 1 (The Worst!)
❑ 2 (Okay)
❑ 3 (The Best)

14 Movie binge at the multiplex
- ❑ 1 (The Worst!)
- ❑ 2 (Okay)
- ❑ 3 (The Best)

15 A long bike ride
- ❑ 1 (The Worst!)
- ❑ 2 (Okay)
- ❑ 3 (The Best)

16 A visit to a psychic
- ❑ 1 (The Worst!)
- ❑ 2 (Okay)
- ❑ 3 (The Best)

17 Hanging in the school yard
- ❑ 1 (The Worst!)
- ❑ 2 (Okay)
- ❑ 3 (The Best)

18 Amusement park
- ❑ 1 (The Worst!)
- ❑ 2 (Okay)
- ❑ 3 (The Best)

19 Baby-sitting
- ❑ 1 (The Worst!)
- ❑ 2 (Okay)
- ❑ 3 (The Best)

20 Making cookies
- ❑ 1 (The Worst!)
- ❑ 2 (Okay)
- ❑ 3 (The Best)

SCORING

If you rated 2, 13, 16, 18, as the best, you like to spend your time doing offbeat, unpredictable things.

3, 5, 7, 9, 15: You're sporty and active and love dates filled with energy.

8, 10, 12, 19, 20: You're so gone on him, even the most ordinary things seem like fun.

4, 6, 11, 14, 17: Your social life could use a little spicing up.

Bonus to everyone who rated 1 as the best: You're pretty normal if you're with your special honey.

chapter FOUR
ALL ABOUT YOU

Lots of times, we're so gone on a guy, we lose sight of someone important—ourselves. Most of all, teen dating is a time that's supposed to be fun but sort of educational—like a prep course where we learn what really turns us on and how to turn others on. The truth is, in this time of your life, there may be bumps along the way, but that happens to everyone, no matter how gorgeous, awesome, or brainy they might be (or how well they cover it up!).

So stop wondering when the phone is going to ring and think about some serious stuff, like "What's Your Romance Style?" or "When Do You Tell Your Friends about Your New Guy?"

what's your
romance style?

When you dress to turn him on, what's your style? Match the entries in the list on the left to one of the three categories on the right.

	Nature Girl	Sex Kitten	Princess
Rosewater perfume	___	___	___
Angora sweaters	___	___	___
Lace-up sandals	___	___	___
Chamomile body lotion	___	___	___
Cashmere anything	___	___	___
L. L. Bean catalog	___	___	___
Leather shorts	___	___	___
Designer slides	___	___	___
Low-slung blue jeans	___	___	___
Manolo Blahnik ankle-strap stilettos	___	___	___

	Nature Girl	Sex Kitten	Princess
Tiffany catalog	____	____	____
Large hoop earrings	____	____	____
Diamond studs	____	____	____
Chanel #5	____	____	____
Tank tops	____	____	____
Beaded bags	____	____	____
Aviator sunglasses	____	____	____
Wide leather belts	____	____	____
Lace-up jeans	____	____	____
Skimpy tops	____	____	____
Hot T-shirts	____	____	____
Dark black eyeliner	____	____	____
Victoria's Secret catalog	____	____	____
Michael Kors perfume	____	____	____
Feather boa	____	____	____
Cotton knits	____	____	____

ANSWERS

Nature Girl	Sex Kitten	Princess
Rosewater perfume	Black eyeliner	Tiffany catalog
Cotton knits	Feather boa	Manolo Blahnik stilettos
L. L. Bean catalog	Lace-up jeans	Designer slides
Chamomile body lotion	Skimpy tops	Cashmere anything
Low-slung blue jeans	Leather shorts	Michael Kors perfume
Tank tops	Victoria's Secret catalog	Diamond studs
Aviator sunglasses	Angora sweaters	Chanel #5
	Large hoop earrings	
	Lace-up sandals	
	Beaded bags	
	Wide leather belts	
	Hot T-shirts	

ARE YOU A **DATING DIVA** OR GIRL'S BEST FRIEND?

Would you rather be out with a guy or rolling with your girls—or is there room for both in a teen's life? Take this quiz to see how skillful you are at blending your boy with your buds. Write in your answers below.

1 If you got upset, would you call your boyfriend or your best friend?

_____

_____

_____

2 On Fridays, do you prefer to go out with your man or party with the girls?

_____

_____

_____

3 The movie you've been waiting months for is finally opening, do you take your guy or the gals?

_____
_____
_____

4 Your English class just got canceled and you have a free hour, who do you go look for? Your girlfriends or boyfriend?

_____
_____
_____

5 Would you rather be at the dance with him or at home having a supergirly slumber party?

_____
_____
_____

6 Do you "dress to impress" more than three times a week for school?

_____
_____
_____

7 Before a weekly party on Saturday night, do you spend more than an hour getting ready?

_____

_____

_____

8 When shopping for that special prom dress, do you go for the one that looks hot but is uncomfortably small, or the one that fits best?

_____

_____

_____

9 If you promised to go to one of his lacrosse games, but your friend failed her driving test and needed a pep talk, which would you do?

_____

_____

_____

10 After school, do you go home with your guy or the girls?

_____

_____

_____

ANSWERS

1. When tears flow and you're upset, who you first call can be a great indication of where your loyalties lie. If you call your best friend, most likely you feel more comfortable with her, but if you call your guy, it shows a strong allegiance to him.

2. Your answer to this indicates who you want to party with. Parties can be some of the most fun and who you choose to spend those good times with is important.

3. If you are really pumped about a new flick coming out, taking your girls can be the best. But this also depends on the type of movie. If it is romantic, a night out with your man could be euphoric, while a lighthearted comedy might serve well for the ladies. A chick-flick is always a great girl-bonder!

4. When you get some unexpected free time, how you spend it is crucial. If you head to the locker room to meet your guy before practice, it is most likely you favor him over a gossip session with the girls.

5. Do you prefer bonding with him or the girls? This question shows whether you'd rather boogie down with him or pounce around with a pillow fight with the ladies.

6. If you feel like you are dressing to impress more than three times a week, it shows how much you want to emphasize looking great.

7. If you are obsessing for over an hour getting ready, you may be having a bonding primping session with the gals—in which case, turn up the music and have fun. If you're freaking out for your guy, you must really want to impress him.

8. If you are more obsessed with the dress that looks hot for him rather than comfort, watch out—popping out on the dance floor won't be the most graceful move all night. Take your most critical girlfriends with you when you shop. They'll tell you which looks best, and you can incorporate your comfort level for the final selection.

9. If you ditched your man to help out a girlfriend in distress, that should be no prob—especially since he'll have more games and she will, it is hoped, fail her driver's test only once.

10. When the pressures from school disappear with the ringing of the final bell, who you go home with is essential. Try to mix it up. Go home some days with him but make sure to single out days for the girls, too.

when do you **tell your friends** about your **new guy?**

Are you top-secret when it comes to your new love or are you the 'tell all' gossip? Take this quiz to find out if you know when to stay silent and when it's time to break the news.

■ ■

1 **You smooch after class. Your first call is**

__**a.** home, making sure you aren't late.

__**b.** speed dial to your friends for a conference call.

__**c.** not made until you get home—you want to sit and savor this moment.

2 **When the rumor spreads that your guy is going to ask you out, you**

__**a.** deny, deny, deny.

__**b.** say, "Well, duh, we are together."

__**c.** say, "We'll see."

3 **At his game, he winks at you during half-time. You**

__**a.** look away, hoping no one saw.

__**b.** say, "Oh my gosh, did you all see that?"

__**c.** play it cool.

♥ ♥ ♥

4 **He calls to come over to hang out. You tell the girls you can't meet them at the diner because**

__**a.** you have to drive your brother to soccer.

__**b.** the hottest guy in school, your new BF, is coming over.

__**c.** something came up—you'll call them later.

♥ ♥ ♥

5 **Your mom asks why you're baking cookies, you reply:**

__**a.** "There's nothing to eat in this house!"

__**b.** "They're for the guy of my dreams."

__**c.** "They're for the school bake sale."

6 **At the movies with the gang, you sit**

___ **a.** two away from him.

___ **b.** next to him, holding hands.

___ **c.** together, but keep the personal space.

♥ ♥ ♥

7 **The girls say they spotted you flirting in class, you say:**

___ **a.** "It was just about that killer chemistry problem."

___ **b.** "He asked me out! Can you believe it?"

___ **c.** "It was nothing, just some innocent chitchat."

♥ ♥ ♥

8 **The girls catch you with a pic of him in your locker. You**

___ **a.** insist he lost it and you are just waiting to see him to return it.

___ **b.** tell them he gave it to you and now it's part of your personal shrine.

___ **c.** say, "You just saw it now?"

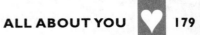

9 In front of your friends, he offers you a ride home. You

__**a.** say, "No thanks."

__**b.** jump in, and promise to call with details when you get home.

__**c.** say, "Sure, but can the girls come along?"

♥ ♥ ♥

10 When you and he get nominated for prom king and queen, you tell the girls:

__**a.** "It must be a joke. We're not together!"

__**b.** "We have to win."

__**c.** "I can't imagine who voted for us."

SCORING

Mostly A's: TIGHT LIPS

You are a top-secret undercover agent and this case is closed. Unfortunately, keeping every detail on the low is a sign of denial. Just be sure that he doesn't get the wrong idea. Sometimes hiding him might be a sign you're embarrassed about your love or insecure about yourself.

Mostly B's: GABBY GIRL

Details? Yes, please! You love to share every intimate detail. You may be excited about first-kiss bliss, but be sure to keep some things private between you and your man. He's dating you, after all, not your friends, and it is important to keep it that way.

Mostly C's: GOOD TALKER

You have a great sense of what is appropriate to share and what should be kept private. Your personal side keeps those intimate, special moments just between you and your guy—while your public side lets you entice your friends with little details here and there.

ARE YOU **intimidated** BY GUYS?

Okay, so in the past, women took a backseat to men—letting them call the shots—but is that really true today? Are you so head over heels in love with a guy that you won't say or do anything to rock your love boat? Or are you just naturally obliging?

If it's important to you to please your squeeze and still get all the good things you deserve, read on. Review column A and match the appropriate response in column B to the situation:

Column A

____**1.** You've just caught your guy nuzzling in the bleachers with the awesome new girl.

____**2.** He decides you're going to the new sci-fi movie even though you're expected at your brother's guitar recital.

Column B

a. After class, ask him to stop.

b. Shrug it off as friendliness.

c. Tell him it's his responsibility.

d. Surprise him with something new.

Column A

____**3.** He screwed up his history paper and now he's blaming you.

____**4.** The notes he keeps slipping you in class are beginning to bug you.

____**5.** When you have an argument, he holds a grudge.

____**6.** He thinks you "look fat" in your new body-hugging sweater.

____**7.** He says he wants to see other girls, but still wants to see you, too.

____**8.** You hate his cologne.

____**9.** His old girlfriend still calls him.

____**10.** You let him do most of the talking.

Column B

e. Say you agree it's time to see other people.

f. Apologize, then do all his homework.

g. Grin and bear it.

h. Keep your family as a priority.

i. Never disagree.

j. Ask yourself if he's insecure.

k. Ask him to buy you another.

l. Tell him more about yourself.

m. Go back to being "just friends."

n. Ignore it.

o. Ask him why he tells you.

p. Being in the background is fine.

q. Apologize over and over.

r. Explain that it bothers you.

s. Go along with whatever he says.

t. Make it a point to assert yourself.

ANSWERS

1. E
2. H
3. C
4. A
5. R
6. K
7. M
8. D
9. O
10. T

how well do
YOU LISTEN TO
RELATIONSHIP SIGNALS?

When it comes to reading signs of a relationship, are you clued in or clueless? Do you always know when things are on the right track or if they are heading downhill? Take this quiz and find out if you are tuning in to the right signals!

---

1 **When your guy says it is over, you hear:**

__**a.** "Time to move on."

__**b.** "It's not over. He's not breaking up with me."

__**c.** "Maybe we can salvage some sort of friendship."

2 **He says, "We need to talk," and you say:**

__**a.** "I'll clear out the afternoon."

__**b.** "Okay, honey, maybe later or this weekend."

__**c.** "Uh-oh, not good times for sure!"

3 **Rumors are flying that he's cheating, you**

_**a.** confront him and ask him straight out what the deal is.

_**b.** say, "Never, he wouldn't cheat on me."

_**c.** wait to hear some more, then go to him.

♥ ♥ ♥

4 **When he's talking, you've been known to**

_**a.** look him in the eye.

_**b.** watch TV and chew gum.

_**c.** let your eyes wander the room and check your watch.

♥ ♥ ♥

5 **He mentions the prom but then seems to lose interest. You**

_**a.** ask him if he is still interested in going.

_**b.** just assume he'll bring it up again.

_**c.** wait a bit, then forget about it.

6 **When your boyfriend seems sad on the phone but says he's "fine," you**

__**a.** go over just to make sure.

__**b.** get mad that he won't tell you what's bothering him.

__**c.** call later to check in.

♥ ♥ ♥

7 **Lately, he's been canceling plans at the last minute. You wonder:**

__**a.** "Maybe he is losing interest."

__**b.** "Oh my gosh, he's cheating on me!"

__**c.** "What am I doing wrong?"

♥ ♥ ♥

8 **You spend lots of time with his buds but he rarely hangs with your girls. You assume**

__**a.** maybe he is hesitant to be around your buddies.

__**b.** he hates your friends.

__**c.** you're ready to share the time, so should he.

9 He wants some space after a bad breakup before getting involved. You think

__**a.** you're interested in more than just being his girlfriend and tell him you'll wait.

__**b.** this stinks—he must be an emotional wimp.

__**c.** maybe he'll get over her and then you can move in for the kill.

♥ ♥ ♥

10 Your friends say he has a bad rep, but he swears his slate is clean. You

__**a.** take their advice and wait for him to make the next move.

__**b.** think, that's right—you're just another one of his girls.

__**c.** tell him it is time for him to prove himself.

SCORING

Mostly A's: CLUED IN

You can always read a situation loud and clear. You listen well and know when to take action. You respect your relationships and are willing to give them the benefit of the doubt on most occasions.

Mostly B's: CLUELESS

Tune in, girlfriend, you are overanalyzing and over-reacting way too often. Take a chill and forget the little things. Hear him out if he wants to talk and let him know you are willing to compromise to make it work.

Mostly C's: STILL TUNING

Sometimes you find the right frequency and get the message, but lots of times you're way off. Make sure you think before you act and don't waste a lot of your own time.

ARE YOUR LOOKS
helping YOU?

Wasn't it the Scottish poet Robert Burns who crystallized the notion of seeing ourselves as others see us? We don't think he was talking about three-way mirrors, but more about the whole package—they way you carry yourself, how you dress, what others perceive your character to be. Whatever—if you're as appearance-obsessed as the rest of us, take this quiz. In it, we'll examine how looks can help reel in your loves—or send them scurrying away.

■ ■

1 Does your everyday makeup routine consist of

___**a.** foundation, powder, concealer, eyeliner, lip liner, lipstick, and blush?

___**b.** a dab of sun block?

___**c.** a little eye shadow, some mascara, and a coat of lip gloss?

2 In the morning, do you

___**a.** spend thirty minutes blow-drying your hair, even if you are just going to the supermarket?

___**b.** sometimes dry your hair, sometimes let it go natural and secure it with some fun clips?

___**c.** wash it and maybe comb it?

3 Are your nails

___**a.** so long and manicured that you have actually been called "Dragon Lady"?

___**b.** nicely trimmed and painted a fun color or with some clear gloss?

___**c.** bitten down to the stumps?

4 When asked at a school basketball game to wear a T-shirt to support the boys, do you reply:

___**a.** "Excuse me, that T-shirt doesn't go with my shoes."

___**b.** "Sure thing," and slip it on over your sweater.

___**c.** "Um, I guess," and take off the stained, holey shirt you are wearing and put on the T-shirt.

5 Is your daily jewelry

__**a.** always rings, bracelets, a necklace, an anklet, earrings, and a toe ring?

__**b.** a silver bangle and a fun necklace, and maybe some rings if they match your outfit?

__**c.** a falling-apart friendship bracelet that you made at camp in sixth grade?

6 Are your gym clothes

__**a.** a matching warm-up pants/T-shirt set and brand-new sneakers every month?

__**b.** a pair of old sweatpants and a T-shirt from your favorite vacation place?

__**c.** the same as the clothes you have been wearing all day–after all, if the teacher doesn't realize you always wear old, crummy clothes, why should you bother to change?

7 Are the shoes you wear most often

__**a.** stacked platform patent leather sandals?

__**b.** a pair of Dr. Martens?

__**c.** old Nikes?

8 When talking to friends in the hall, are you

___**a.** talking while reapplying lip liner?

___**b.** chatting casually?

___**c.** standing slouched over and staring at the floor?

9 In class, do you

___**a.** spend the whole time listening to voice mail messages on your cell phone and changing the settings?

___**b.** sit there and exchange a few eye rolls when the teacher gets really boring?

___**c.** look at the desk and pick at your mosquito bites?

10 Is your schoolbag

___**a.** a leather designer bag filled with toiletries?

___**b.** a messenger bag or regular backpack with a few notebooks?

___**c.** your old, ink-stained bag that is torn in several places from having been shoved into your locker so many times?

ANSWERS

Mostly A's: SURFACE GIRL

Whoa! How are there possibly enough hours in the day for you to fit your look into your schedule? You give off the impression of being overly concerned with your appearance, something guys don't like. Try to tone it down a little. Going casual can be fun and a lot less hassle.

Mostly B's: GUY GETTER

Good job! You know how to look slammin' without going over the top. People will appreciate your simple style and classy ways. Boys go for girls who know how to look good without living in front of the mirror.

Mostly C's: MAKEOVER MAMA

You need to catch up with the others. Try to find a happy medium where you can look a little more plugged into the social scene. It's a rare guy who finds sloppy attractive.

SURVIVOR:
can you get over being dumped?

Anyone who's ever been dumped knows it's no fun. Besides the first quick hit, there are always aftershocks to bring you down. There are, however, ways to speed your total recovery. Let's see how expert you are at diagnosing the right moves to get you beyond that ton-of-bricks feeling and back onto the love track—which we know won't be long!

Check "Healthy One" for a move that's healing, "Suffering Sister" for one that only prolongs the misery:

■ ■

1 Dishing the breakup with your buds—once
❑ **Healthy One**
❑ **Suffering Sister**

2 Going on a weeklong Ben & Jerry's binge
❑ **Healthy One**
❑ **Suffering Sister**

3 Staying home from places where you and your crush used to hang
❑ Healthy One
❑ Suffering Sister

4 Calling up old friends to catch up
❑ Healthy One
❑ Suffering Sister

5 Thinking it was all "your fault"
❑ Healthy One
❑ Suffering Sister

6 Hitting the mall for cool new clothes
❑ Healthy One
❑ Suffering Sister

7 Flirting at the next party
❑ Healthy One
❑ Suffering Sister

8 Trading in your baggy sweats and T-shirt for body-hugging workout clothes
❑ Healthy One
❑ Suffering Sister

9 Making plans for Saturday night
❑ Healthy One
❑ Suffering Sister

10 Grooving on daytime TV
❑ Healthy One
❑ Suffering Sister

11 Blowing off family plans so you can be alone and mope
❑ Healthy One
❑ Suffering Sister

12 Keeping sexy snapshots of him in your drawer
❑ Healthy One
❑ Suffering Sister

13 Asking his buds about him
❑ Healthy One
❑ Suffering Sister

14 Going out of your way to keep connections alive, like dropping off his term papers for him
❑ Healthy One
❑ Suffering Sister

15 Referring to him as "my ex"
❑ Healthy One
❑ Suffering Sister

16 Playing your favorite "couple" songs
❑ Healthy One
❑ Suffering Sister

17 Staying cool when you do see him
❑ Healthy One
❑ Suffering Sister

18 Thinking he actually did you a favor
❑ Healthy One
❑ Suffering Sister

19 Planning a family outing
❑ Healthy One
❑ Suffering Sister

20 Staying unattached for a while

❏ Healthy One
❏ Suffering Sister

21 Looking good all day—every day

❏ Healthy One
❏ Suffering Sister

22 Not bitching to his new girl

❏ Healthy One
❏ Suffering Sister

23 Starting a new exercise routine

❏ Healthy One
❏ Suffering Sister

24 Looking unfazed

❏ Healthy One
❏ Suffering Sister

25 Ransacking his locker for "your stuff"

❏ Healthy One
❏ Suffering Sister

26 Wondering what you saw in him anyway

❏ Healthy One
❏ Suffering Sister

SCORING

1. Healthy	10. Suffering	19. Healthy
2. Suffering	11. Suffering	20. Healthy
3. Suffering	12. Suffering	21. Healthy
4. Healthy	13. Suffering	22. Healthy
5 Suffering	14. Suffering	23. Healthy
6. Healthy	15. Suffering	24. Healthy
7. Healthy	16. Suffering	25. Suffering
8. Healthy	17. Healthy	26. Suffering
9. Healthy	18. Healthy	

More Suffering Signs than Healthy?

Girl, let go of that loser head. Don't make it worse by keeping bad feelings alive. Do yourself a big favor and remember you're special—show your stuff by staying together. Life promises you many more chances at romance.

More Healthy Signs than Suffering?

You're cool and you know how to handle yourself. Your self-esteem is A+, and it will keep you the winner you are.

can YOU SPOT a player?

Players are like tornadoes in Kansas—leveling everything in sight, especially tender teen hearts. If you're wondering about a certain guy and his ability on the "playing field," take this quiz to find out if he's a serial Ladies Man, yanking your chain, or a Sweetie, keeping it real!

Check off the ones that apply to your man. Add or subtract points where applicable.

■■■■■■■■■■■■■■■■■■■■■■■■■■■■■

___ **1** Has he ever called you someone else's name?
(Yes, add 1 point. Add 2 points if it was a girl's.)

___ **2** Does he pay full attention to you when you're alone and then ignore you in public?
(Yes, add 1 point.)

___ **3** Is he known to "get around"?
(Yes, add 1 point.)

___ **4** Do girls call him "Don Juan"?
(Yes, add 1 point.)

___ **5** Is his number on the girl's bathroom wall?
(Yes, add 1 point. Add 2 points if it's in more than one stall.)

___ **6** When you see him at the football game, do his friends move over so you can sit together?
(Yes, subtract 1 point. Add 1 point if no.)

___ **7** Has he referred to you as his girlfriend?
(Yes, subtract 1 point. Add 1 point if no.)

___ **8** In public, will he ever put his arm around you?
(Yes, subtract 1 point. Add 1 point if no.)

___ **9** Does he still say you're beautiful even when you have a huge zit?
(Yes, subtract 1 point. Add 2 points if no.)

___ **10** Is he known to call girls "sweet lips" or "hottie"?
(Add 1 point for each yes.)

___ **11** When you send him a note, does he recognize your handwriting?
(Yes, subtract 1 point. Add 1 point if no.)

___ **12** On your Valentine card, does he sign "Love, me"?
(Yes, subtract 1 point. Add 1 point if no.)

___ **13** Does he wait after your games to drive you home?
(Yes, subtract 1 point. Add one point if no.)

___ **14** Have you caught him giving a girl "friend" a massage?
(Yes, add 1 point.)

___ **15** Has he ever made you a mix tape?
(Yes, subtract 2 points. Add 1 point if no.)

SCORING

1-2 POINTS

He is a total sweetie and he's not afraid to show it in front of his friends, his family, or in public. He is into you and wants to "keep it real." No mind games here, so stick with this guy and you will have a great love connection.

3-5 POINTS

This guy may be confused. While on one hand he seems misleading with his conniving tactics, on the other he still is sweet to you at times. Make sure to watch him carefully—he may be playing games with your heart.

6-10 POINTS

Total player. This guy is a big-time loser. He is playing mind games and his reputation shows how he wants to get around with as many as possible. While he might have feelings for you, who wants a guy who flirts with every girl in the place? Get rid of this guy and find someone who will be straight with you!

can you CONSOLE your sweetie?

Do you know how to soothe your main squeeze? Can you cheer him out of the deepest emotional ditch? Take this quiz to find out if you can nurse him back to a smile!

Check yes or no if the move will cheer him up or not.

	YES	NO
1 He gets in a fight with his dad, so you offer to let him sleep on your couch.	____	____
2 He fails his bio midterm, so you promise to tutor him for the final.	____	____
3 He's sick with a cold, so you steer clear to avoid the bug.	____	____

YES   NO

4 He has the sniffles, so you head over with a box of supersoft tissues and a bottle of vitamin C.   ____ ____

5 He's bumming 'cause his fave team lost. You tell him to grow up and get over it.   ____ ____

6 He's raging against his mom for taking away his car. To play peacemaker, you offer to drive him to school.   ____ ____

7 He lost his favorite sweater. You say, "Hey, you're lucky—it's only a sweater. I lost my wallet last year."   ____ ____

8 His parakeet flew the coop. You tell him how cruel it is to cage up birds and animals.   ____ ____

9 He missed the lead in the play and he's devastated. Do you tell him to go for the understudy?   ____ ____

10 He misses his sister at college. Do you bring over a care package of stamps, stationery, and phone cards?   ____ ____

ANSWERS

1. Yes	6. Yes
2. Yes	7. No
3. No	8. No
4. Yes	9. Yes
5. No	10. Yes

Mostly Right: SENSITIVE SWEETIE

You know just how to console your man when he feels blue. You support him and that helps him pull through tough times. Keep up the great work and remember, he appreciates all the little things you do.

Mostly Wrong: WARM UP

He needs your help. Especially in a time of loss, depression, or sadness, support from a close friend is essential. Try to think of how he would react if the roles were reversed. A little consideration will go a long way.

chapter FIVE
STICKY SITUATIONS

While this chapter may be short, it's loaded with tough issues. Cupid doesn't always shoot his arrow straight into your heart—sometimes it lands in our brains, leaving us clueless as to what's really going on. While we hope these delicate situations don't happen to you, we urge you to test your skills in case you're ever needed to perform CPR on a friend's teenage heart.

"HELP! I'm involved with **two guys** at once!"

Are you digging yourself into a hole the size of a soccer field? Being the center of two guys' attention is fun, but you could also be making a huge mistake. Take this quiz to find out if two is twice as much fun—or double trouble!

- -

Check off the appropriate answer:

1 Do you regularly date two guys at once?
❏ YES ❏ NO ❏ SOMETIMES

2 Have you kissed two guys in one night before?
❏ YES ❏ NO ❏ SOMETIMES

3 Do the two guys know about your "arrangement"?
❏ YES ❏ NO ❏ SOMETIMES

4 If not, are you feeling overwhelmed by the stress of keeping your excuses straight?
❏ YES ❏ NO ❏ SOMETIMES

5 And, are you constantly screening your calls when one guy is over?
❑ YES ❑ NO ❑ SOMETIMES

6 Do the guys have other "loves," too?
❑ YES ❑ NO ❑ SOMETIMES

7 Would you ever think about lying to your guy to cover up another hookup?
❑ YES ❑ NO ❑ SOMETIMES

8 Are you feeling confused?
❑ YES ❑ NO ❑ SOMETIMES

9 Do you usually get bored with just one guy?
❑ YES ❑ NO ❑ SOMETIMES

10 Have you done this before?
❑ YES ❑ NO ❑ SOMETIMES

11 Do you like to play hard to get with most guys?
❑ YES ❑ NO ❑ SOMETIMES

12 Do you need to be the center of attention?
❑ YES ❑ NO ❑ SOMETIMES

13 Is dating really a game to you?
❑ YES ❑ NO ❑ SOMETIMES

14 Do you like having one man long distance and one close to home?
❑ YES ❑ NO ❑ SOMETIMES

15 Does dating more than one guy make you feel in charge?
❑ YES ❑ NO ❑ SOMETIMES

16 Are you known to have crushed on many people at once?
❑ YES ❑ NO ❑ SOMETIMES

17 Do your friends know?
❑ YES ❑ NO ❑ SOMETIMES

18 Do they think it's cool?
❑ YES ❑ NO ❑ SOMETIMES

SCORING

MOSTLY "YES"

Troublesome Twos: *Beware!* Tempting yourself may seem like a fun game, but it can lead to major heartache and a lonely existence. Your lies and deceit may leave you without either guy if you haven't told them. Be careful because you may hurt both guys and yourself.

MOSTLY "NO"

You realize the hazards with trying to get involved with two hearts at once. Steer clear of the sticky frustrations and claim one guy. If you are unsure, wait it out until you know which one you really want and then go for it! Basic rule: Play it safe—one guy!

MOSTLY "SOMETIMES"

While you may have some tempting thoughts about being the center of attention and wanting to date two guys, you also understand the possible repercussions. If you're between real loves, your love triangle isn't such a healthy place for long. Keep it cool and focus on the one you want—you'll be better off in the end.

"SHOULD I **get involved** with SOMEONE I WORK WITH?"

Do you volunteer at a local hospital or work summers at your town camp? Whatever your work situation, a lot of times temptation will be lurking in the form of some good-looking guy who pays attention to you. But is it a good idea to mix business with pleasure? How would you rate your on-the-job love training?

Check the answer you most agree with:

1 He's eight years older than you are but asked you out anyway. It feels a little creepy. Should you go?
❑ YES   ❑ NO   ❑ SOMETIMES

2 The director's son keeps lurking around saying that he wants you to go out with him. Can you just say no?
❑ YES   ❑ NO   ❑ SOMETIMES

3 Camp is a blast. You know some of the guy counselors have girlfriends, but they're always huggy and flirty. Should you resist?
❑ YES   ❑ NO   ❑ SOMETIMES

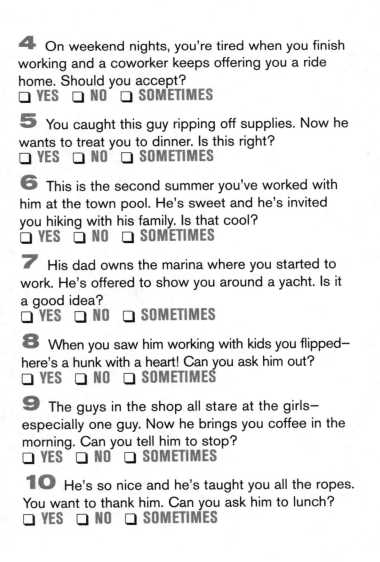

4 On weekend nights, you're tired when you finish working and a coworker keeps offering you a ride home. Should you accept?
❑ YES ❑ NO ❑ SOMETIMES

5 You caught this guy ripping off supplies. Now he wants to treat you to dinner. Is this right?
❑ YES ❑ NO ❑ SOMETIMES

6 This is the second summer you've worked with him at the town pool. He's sweet and he's invited you hiking with his family. Is that cool?
❑ YES ❑ NO ❑ SOMETIMES

7 His dad owns the marina where you started to work. He's offered to show you around a yacht. Is it a good idea?
❑ YES ❑ NO ❑ SOMETIMES

8 When you saw him working with kids you flipped— here's a hunk with a heart! Can you ask him out?
❑ YES ❑ NO ❑ SOMETIMES

9 The guys in the shop all stare at the girls— especially one guy. Now he brings you coffee in the morning. Can you tell him to stop?
❑ YES ❑ NO ❑ SOMETIMES

10 He's so nice and he's taught you all the ropes. You want to thank him. Can you ask him to lunch?
❑ YES ❑ NO ❑ SOMETIMES

ANSWERS

1. No—eight years is a big age difference, especially when you're young.

2. Yes. He's taking advantage of his family position.

3. Yes—don't get too physical. You'll just be something on the side.

4. No—never take a ride in a car until you're totally certain it's safe.

5. No way—he's trying to buy your silence. Ignore him.

6. Yes—that's a healthy way to get to know him.

7. No—it's way too private and intimate. Wait until you know him better.

8. Sure—try asking him for coffee first.

9. Yes—politely tell him you always get your own.

10. Yes—why not bring a picnic lunch and take him to a nearby park?

are your **parents** **meddling** with your **love life?**

It's as inevitable as final exams—during your relationship with a guy, there will always come a time when the parents assert themselves. Whether they've already given you lots of ground rules or proceed on a case-by-case basis, there will be limits. In the quiz below mark the answer that best fits your situation:

▪▪▪▪▪▪▪▪▪▪▪▪▪▪▪▪▪▪▪▪▪▪▪▪▪▪▪▪▪▪

1 **Their idea of a curfew is**

__**a.** workable.

__**b.** way too early.

__**c.** nonexistent.

2 **Before you roll with your guy, Dad says**

__**a.** "Be careful."

__**b.** "Change those clothes!"

__**c.** "Don't forget to pick up dog food."

3 Before accepting a big date, do you have to ask permission?

__**a.** Never.

__**b.** Always.

__**c.** If you have to buy an expensive outfit.

4 Mom wants to go with you to shop for a prom dress. You think

__**a.** her style belongs in the Smithsonian.

__**b.** she'll always steer you to a slammin' outfit.

__**c.** she'll pay.

5 How often do the 'rents insist on meeting your squeeze?

__**a.** Most of the time.

__**b.** Always.

__**c.** They don't care.

6 Dad gives off what date vibe?

__**a.** "Have fun!"

__**b.** "The Secret Service will be watching you."

__**c.** "Don't do what I did."

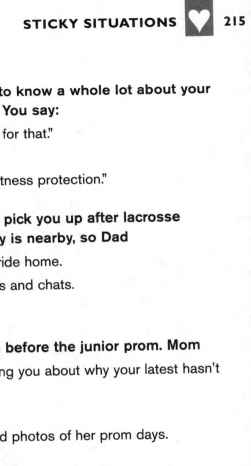

7 Mom wants to know a whole lot about your new guy's family. You say:

__**a.** "It's too early for that."

__**b.** "Chill!"

__**c.** "They're in witness protection."

8 Dad likes to pick you up after lacrosse practice. Your boy is nearby, so Dad

__**a.** offers him a ride home.

__**b.** shakes hands and chats.

__**c.** stares.

9 It's a month before the junior prom. Mom

__**a.** keeps bugging you about why your latest hasn't asked.

__**b.** acts cool.

__**c.** brings out old photos of her prom days.

10 After meeting your guy, Dad and Mom

__**a.** constantly discuss him.

__**b.** always ask where he is.

__**c.** wait for you to bring his name up.

ANSWERS

1. When you're starting to date, most parents make you punch a time clock. If you said A or C, they're probably trusting. B—or "way too early"— could be temporary. They might loosen up as you get older.

2. A: Dad's custodial and caring.
   B: He's worrying about you.
   C: He's very laid back.

3. A: You've got a free pass, girl.
   B: If it's starting to choke you, why not tell them?
   C: If you expect the 'rents to spring for that new outfit, you'd better clear it in advance.

4. B and C make for successful shopping. Pick A and you should be showing her some recent magazines.

5. A and B are normal. C can give him the wrong impression.

6. A: Dad's cool.
   B: He's overboard with the protection.
   C: He's typical.

7. A: If your romance is lasting, feed the 'rents more info.

8. A: Dad wants to check out where the young crush lives.
    B: He wants to be friendly.
    C: He's acting like a jerk.

9. B means Mother knows best. A and C, she's rubbing salt into the wound.

10. By making him topic A, they could be making you sick of him. Ask them to chill a little. C is the way to go.

are you **worried** he's **abusive?**

What is abuse anyway? It can be emotional, where your feelings get hurt too much; or physical, where your body actually gets hurt; or mental, where your head gets too pushed around. If you're feeling bad about any of these things, talk to a friend, teacher, or parent. Remember, guys should make you feel good—but what's most important are the limits you set about how others treat you and the way you treat yourself.

■ ■

How would you describe these situations?

	ABUSIVE	NORMAL
1 Stands you up a lot	_____	_____
2 Forgets your birthday	_____	_____
3 Tells other guys personal things about you	_____	_____
4 Gossips about your family	_____	_____

	ABUSIVE	NORMAL
5 Expects you to pay for lots of things	_____	_____
6 Smokes around you	_____	_____
7 Hints that he wants expensive presents	_____	_____
8 Wants you to do things you don't want to do	_____	_____
9 Acts rude to you in public	_____	_____
10 Avoids your family	_____	_____
11 Makes jokes about you	_____	_____
12 Calls you crummy nicknames like "Jughead" and "Klutz"	_____	_____
13 Drives too fast	_____	_____
14 Ducks out when you have heavy chores to do	_____	_____
15 Puts his schedule first	_____	_____
16 Keeps you waiting	_____	_____

	ABUSIVE	**NORMAL**
17 Jokes that you're too fat	_____	_____
18 Tells you you're lucky to be with him	_____	_____
19 Goes into your wallet without asking	_____	_____
20 Blows up, then apologizes later	_____	_____
21 Fools around behind your back	_____	_____
22 Monopolizes your time when you have schoolwork to do	_____	_____
23 Never congratulates you on a job well done	_____	_____
24 Always takes care of himself first	_____	_____
25 Doesn't refer to you as his girlfriend	_____	_____

ANSWERS

All of these situations are undesirable behavior. It's okay for guys to tease, but put-downs are out. Unkind names, rudeness, and lack of respect have no place in teen love. Now's the time to be getting all the good things and having fun. If you know someone who's suffering from a fool, help her get out of a bad situation.

"YIKES! My Family **hates** Him!"
Can True Romance Prevail?

Is your main squeeze now the butt of family jokes? Does Dad have more nicknames for him than for the dog? And, are they not even bothering to hide their feelings?

Rate each situation:

1 Dad caught your guy smoking in your powder room.
- ❏ BAD
- ❏ REALLY BAD
- ❏ FORGET IT

2 Your guy told Mom her hairdo made her look "younger."
- ❏ BAD
- ❏ REALLY BAD
- ❏ FORGET IT

3 They won't invite him over during the holidays.
- ❏ BAD
- ❏ REALLY BAD
- ❏ FORGET IT

4 Your sister always tells him how wonderful your former boyfriends were.
- ❏ BAD
- ❏ REALLY BAD
- ❏ FORGET IT

5 He's a Yankee fan and the whole family is obsessed with the Mets.
❑ BAD
❑ REALLY BAD
❑ FORGET IT

6 You try telling the 'rents your guy doesn't drink, but Dad always gives him the "no drinking" speech.
❑ BAD
❑ REALLY BAD
❑ FORGET IT

7 Dad has warned him not to wear his nose ring to the house.
❑ BAD
❑ REALLY BAD
❑ FORGET IT

8 Last week, Dad busted him at the drugstore buying "personal items."
❑ BAD
❑ REALLY BAD
❑ FORGET IT

9 Mom never asks him to stay for dinner.
❑ BAD
❑ REALLY BAD
❑ FORGET IT

10 He mowed the lawn and broke the mower.
❑ BAD
❑ REALLY BAD
❑ FORGET IT

11 Mom never has any of his favorite munchies on hand.
❑ BAD
❑ REALLY BAD
❑ FORGET IT

12 When your crush had to go to the hospital after a lacrosse pileup, they didn't ask after him.
❑ BAD
❑ REALLY BAD
❑ FORGET IT

13 Dad found a scratch on his new SUV and accused your boy of making it.
❑ BAD
❑ REALLY BAD
❑ FORGET IT

14 When you try to explain that your crush has good qualities, Dad asks if there could possibly be other guys in school worth your time.
❑ BAD
❑ REALLY BAD
❑ FORGET IT

15 The dog bit him.
❑ BAD
❑ REALLY BAD
❑ FORGET IT

SCORING

You've probably realized all of these are bad—some a lot worse than others. You've got to admit smoking in the house is "really bad" and complimenting Mom in an oafish way is lame and "bad." There may not be a place for your beau at intimate family occasions, but to not invite him rates a "really bad." He is entitled to love a different sports team from your family, but that won't endear him to them. The nose ring issue is tough. Number 9-not asking him to stay for dinner—is a total "forget it." They're not going out of their way at all. Breaking the lawn mower is "bad" but forgivable; however, your parents' not asking about his health is a big "forget it," as is accusing him of scratching Dad's car. Mom doesn't care much if there are no snacks and Dad scores "forget it" for telling you to move on. Sadly, even the dog doesn't like him—he rates a "forget it."

PSYCHED UP OR PSYCHO?
Are You **changing** for a Guy?

Some chicks get so into their crushes and guys, they start to become other people. They may be dropping their buds, changing their attitudes, wardrobes, hairstyles! Can you spot the signs—subtle and otherwise—of a transformation? See how well you do below by rating whether you are just "psyched up" or going "psycho."

■ ■

	PSYCHED UP	PSYCHO
1 Blue is his favorite color. You look dead in it, but you buy a blue necklace.	____	____
2 Every time he calls, you walk around with a cell phone glued to your head.	____	____
3 He mentions how much he digs Britney Spears and suddenly you dye your hair blonde.	____	____

PSYCHED UP PSYCHO

4 You're studious, but he likes to get scene-y, so you've started to stay up late and party. Your grades tank. _____ _____

5 He loves long nails, so even though they inhibit you, you grow them superlong. _____ _____

6 He's a loner, so you start dropping your friends. _____ _____

7 You're a vegetarian; he scarfs up the beef burgers. You've started to wonder, "What's so bad about meat?" _____ _____

8 *Beauty junkie* didn't begin to describe you before you met him—now you wear nothing but cologne because he says it's "more natural." _____ _____

9 You planned to visit with your buds from camp next spring break. Your crush says he'll be around, so you decide to stay home. _____ _____

PSYCHED UP PSYCHO

10 You used to love Motown oldies—now you're developing a newfound love of his fave, rap.

_____ _____

11 You're afraid to disagree with him in public.

_____ _____

12 Helping at the library book sale used to be fun, but he'd rather skip it. So you do.

_____ _____

13 He loves strappy heels, so you blow your savings on a sexy pair of Jimmy Choo's.

_____ _____

ANSWERS

1. "Psyched up": It's normal to wear what pleases him and smart to wear what flatters you. Good work finding a way to combine the two!

2. "Psyched up": Being on the phone incessantly with your guy is supernormal.

3. Radically changing your hair color on a whim for a guy is "psycho." You should want to do something this extreme for yourself.

4. Bagging your studies is bad and "psycho."

5. Trying new things is normal, but if it gets too out there, it becomes "psycho."

6. Never drop your buds for a guy—this is "psycho."

7. Losing your principles is approaching "psycho."

8. Cutting back on the makeup may not be totally bad, but all the way could be "psycho."

9. "Psycho" big-time! First, why would you want him to think you're so available? And second, never drop your good buds on the off chance that a guy will come a-callin'.

10. "Psyched up": It's normal to be open to new things, like music and art.

11. If you're afraid to disagree with him, then you're going "psycho."

12. "Psycho": If he can't see why it's important to help the community, lose him.

13. "Psycho": At this point in your life, you should be more into self-development.